Evil: A Very Short Introduction

T0016645

VERY SHORT INTRODUCTIONS are for anyone wanting a stimulating and accessible way into a new subject. They are written by experts, and have been translated into more than 45 different languages.

The series began in 1995, and now covers a wide variety of topics in every discipline. The VSI library currently contains over 700 volumes—a Very Short Introduction to everything from Psychology and Philosophy of Science to American History and Relativity—and continues to grow in every subject area.

Very Short Introductions available now:

ABOLITIONISM Richard S. Newman
THE ABRAHAMIC RELIGIONS
  Charles L. Cohen
ACCOUNTING Christopher Nobes
ADOLESCENCE Peter K. Smith
THEODOR W. ADORNO
  Andrew Bowie
ADVERTISING Winston Fletcher
AERIAL WARFARE Frank Ledwidge
AESTHETICS Bence Nanay
AFRICAN AMERICAN RELIGION
  Eddie S. Glaude Jr
AFRICAN HISTORY John Parker and
  Richard Rathbone
AFRICAN POLITICS Ian Taylor
AFRICAN RELIGIONS
  Jacob K. Olupona
AGEING Nancy A. Pachana
AGNOSTICISM Robin Le Poidevin
AGRICULTURE Paul Brassley and
  Richard Soffe
ALEXANDER THE GREAT
  Hugh Bowden
ALGEBRA Peter M. Higgins
AMERICAN BUSINESS HISTORY
  Walter A. Friedman
AMERICAN CULTURAL HISTORY
  Eric Avila
AMERICAN FOREIGN RELATIONS
  Andrew Preston
AMERICAN HISTORY
  Paul S. Boyer
AMERICAN IMMIGRATION
  David A. Gerber

AMERICAN INTELLECTUAL
  HISTORY
  Jennifer Ratner-Rosenhagen
THE AMERICAN JUDICIAL SYSTEM
  Charles L. Zelden
AMERICAN LEGAL HISTORY
  G. Edward White
AMERICAN MILITARY HISTORY
  Joseph T. Glatthaar
AMERICAN NAVAL HISTORY
  Craig L. Symonds
AMERICAN POETRY David Caplan
AMERICAN POLITICAL HISTORY
  Donald Critchlow
AMERICAN POLITICAL PARTIES
  AND ELECTIONS L. Sandy Maisel
AMERICAN POLITICS
  Richard M. Valelly
THE AMERICAN PRESIDENCY
  Charles O. Jones
THE AMERICAN REVOLUTION
  Robert J. Allison
AMERICAN SLAVERY
  Heather Andrea Williams
THE AMERICAN SOUTH
  Charles Reagan Wilson
THE AMERICAN WEST Stephen Aron
AMERICAN WOMEN'S HISTORY
  Susan Ware
AMPHIBIANS T. S. Kemp
ANAESTHESIA Aidan O'Donnell
ANALYTIC PHILOSOPHY
  Michael Beaney
ANARCHISM Alex Prichard

Available soon:

For more information visit our website

www.oup.com/vsi/

Luke Russell

EVIL

A Very Short Introduction

OXFORD
UNIVERSITY PRESS

OXFORD
UNIVERSITY PRESS

Great Clarendon Street, Oxford, OX2 6DP,
United Kingdom

Oxford University Press is a department of the University of Oxford.
It furthers the University's objective of excellence in research, scholarship,
and education by publishing worldwide. Oxford is a registered trade mark of
Oxford University Press in the UK and in certain other countries

First published in hardback as Being Evil 2020
First published as a Very Short Introduction 2022

Published in the United States of America by Oxford University Press
198 Madison Avenue, New York, NY 10016, United States of America

British Library Cataloguing in Publication Data
Data available

Library of Congress Control Number: 2022937408

ISBN 978–0–19–881927–1

Printed and bound by
CPI Group (UK) Ltd, Croydon, CR0 4YY

Contents

Chapter 1
The philosophical puzzle of evil

Does evil exist? To answer that question we first have to know what 'evil' means. What do you think of when you hear that word? Is it a stereotypical villain from the movies or from literary fiction—Voldemort from *Harry Potter*, Ramsay Bolton from *Game of Thrones*, or the Emperor from *Star Wars*—the kind who actively seek to destroy others, who delight in inflicting suffering, and who cackle while contemplating their malicious deeds? Perhaps instead you think of superheroes who are called to use their power for good, not evil. Maybe what springs to mind is Google's former corporate motto: Don't be evil. When people use the word 'evil' in these contexts they seem to be indulging in playful hyperbole. Evil is scary and bad, but it is so exaggeratedly scary and bad that there is something unrealistic, even ridiculous, about it. Evil, in this sense, teeters on the edge of the comical. The character of Dr Evil from the *Austen Powers* films steps right over this edge. How silly, how childish, we might say, to be frightened of eeeevil. If we were to focus on examples like these, we might conclude that there is no room for the concept of evil in serious thinking about morality.

For some people the word 'evil' carries a different set of connotations. Rather than belonging in the realm of fiction, it sounds distinctly religious. When we look to Christianity, for example, we find plenty of references to evil. In the Garden of

Eden Adam and Eve ate the forbidden fruit and gained knowledge of good and evil. When Christians say the Lord's Prayer they ask to be delivered from evil. Thomas Aquinas says that we should do good and avoid evil. The idea here seems to be that evil is simply the opposite of good. Elsewhere in Christianity, a more radical—some would say outlandish—conception of evil appears to be in play. The Gospels contain repeated references to Satan, an evil supernatural being who causes illness and enters into the hearts of humans, leading them to sin. The Book of Revelation describes Satan in the form of a giant dragon engaging in a cosmic battle with God. To those of us who do not believe in the existence of God or malevolent spirits, this supernaturalist conception of evil seems to be just as fanciful as the kind of evil that is depicted in *Harry Potter* or *Star Wars*. Moreover, it appears to be dangerous to believe that this kind of supernatural evil exists in the real world. We should not forget the terrifying witch trials of the 17th century, in which thousands of innocent people were tortured and burned at the stake, all because of misguided beliefs in evil spirits and demonic possession. Contemporary politicians who use the language of evil are sometimes accused of fostering exactly this kind of moral atmosphere: of demonizing their opponents, of whipping up the angry mob, of inciting wanton destruction. Some philosophers survey this landscape and conclude that we ought to be sceptical of the existence of evil. Evil seems to be an outdated concept, and a dangerous one, at that.

But should we, on the basis of these examples, rush to the conclusion that evil is not real? According to the philosopher Ludwig Wittgenstein, a common cause of philosophical disease is 'a *one-sided diet*: one nourishes one's thinking with only one kind of example.' Consider an analogy: if you want to understand the nature of politics but you focus only on Western liberal democracies, you will fail to grasp the distinctive features of monarchies, communist states, dictatorships, and so on. Similarly, if you want to understand the nature of music it would be misleading to focus only on heavy metal and simply ignore classical symphonies, African drumming, jazz, and so on. When conducting a philosophical investigation we are best able to gain knowledge by considering a diverse range of cases. Those who hope to understand the nature of evil by focusing only on fantasy, science fiction, and religious texts are consuming just this kind of one-sided diet. Instead of limiting our focus in this way we should also look at the broad range of real-world scenarios in which ordinary people are inclined to use the word 'evil'. Unfortunately this is a grim task and is prone to induce disgust and despair. It is hard to think clearly about the worst moral transgressions in human history. Nonetheless, this is what we must do if we are to figure out what evil is supposed to be, and whether it exists. After considering these examples some of us might still conclude that there is no such thing as evil. It could turn out that people who believe in the existence of evil are falling into some kind of confusion, are exaggerating, or are mistakenly projecting onto the world something that, in reality, is not there. We should not prejudge the matter either way. Let us begin by taking note of what ordinary people say and what they believe about evil, and then we can move on to ask whether their claims and beliefs are correct.

When we survey the wide range of cases in which people say that things are evil, we notice something quite surprising. Sometimes we use the word 'evil' simply as a synonym for 'bad'. When we do so 'evil' need not have any connotations of extremity. Just as there can be minor or trivial bad things, there can be minor or trivial evil things, in this sense of the word. Suppose that you face a dilemma, and you have to choose between two bad options. You might explain your ultimate decision by saying that you chose the lesser of two evils. When you use the word 'evil' in this way, you are not implying that both options were extreme and horrific. You are simply indicating that you chose the least bad of the two. When the word 'evil' is being used merely as a synonym for 'bad' it can be applied to things that are blameworthy moral wrongs, such as malicious assaults, but it can also be applied to things that are bad without being immoral, including the pain that you suffer when you stub your toe. When we consult the *Oxford English Dictionary* to discover the etymology of the word 'evil', we see that it grew from the Old English word 'yfel', meaning 'over' or 'beyond', and that for centuries the word 'evil' was used simply as a synonym for 'bad', 'troublesome', and 'painful'.

These days it might sound odd to use the word 'evil' to mean nothing more than bad. A restaurant critic who gives a negative review is unlikely to say that the food was evil, for instance. Nonetheless, we can find contexts in which this old-fashioned use of the word 'evil' to mean 'bad' persists. This usage will be familiar to anyone who has encountered what philosophers and theologians call the Problem of Evil. The Problem of Evil is a challenge that arises for theists, who believe that the world was created by an all-powerful, all-knowing, and perfectly good God. If this is what God is like, and if God loves us, we might expect that God would create a world filled with good things, in which we would live perfectly happy lives. Yet when we look around us we cannot help but notice that the world contains many bad things. Much suffering is caused by human wrongdoing, and might thus be thought to be our fault, rather than God's fault. Even so, a great deal of undeserved suffering is caused by illnesses, including cancer, arthritis, and tuberculosis. Natural disasters such as earthquakes, tsunamis, and floods take the lives of countless innocent people. Some babies die painful deaths, and their parents' lives are filled with grief. The animal kingdom is also drenched in suffering due to injury, predation, and starvation. The so-called Problem of Evil is the problem of how to reconcile belief in a benevolent and all-powerful God with the knowledge that the world contains so many bad things, or, as it is usually put in this context, so much evil. Many people think that the Problem of Evil gives us a good reason to be atheists. According to this view the ubiquity of undeserved suffering counts as strong evidence that the world was *not* created by an omnipotent, omniscient, and omnibenevolent God. In response theists have tried to explain how it could be that a good God created a world that contains so many bad things.

My aim in this book is not to address the theological Problem of Evil. Nor is it to focus on this maximally broad and inclusive usage of the word 'evil' to mean simply that which is bad. My target is not that which is bad in a non-moral way, such as toothaches and broken bones. Nor is my target that which is morally bad but only trivial or minor. What I aim to understand is that which is not merely bad but *evil*: that which is morally bad or wrong in some extreme sense. This, I believe, is the concept of evil that is in play when philosophers, historians, psychologists, and journalists are arguing about whether evil really exists. Obviously we need to say more about exactly what it means to call something evil in this extreme and moralized sense of the word. I think that we can get a better grip on the concept of evil by returning to consider the things that ordinary people might say are not merely bad, but evil. This time let us keep in mind that there are heated disputes about whether anything really is evil in this more extreme sense. A philosophical analysis of the concept of evil must be able to make sense of the fact that some intelligent and well-informed people believe that evil is real, while others believe that evil is a myth or a dangerous fantasy. If we want to identify the concept of evil that is in play in these disputes we should start by focusing on the contested examples. As we work through these various examples I encourage you to try to keep an open mind. Rather than rushing to judgement, slow down and probe your own thoughts. Think about the similarities between these cases, and see if you can identify any interesting differences between them. Ask yourself whether some are morally worse than others, and whether some share a distinctive feature that marks them out as particularly egregious.

Let us start by looking at terrorism, perhaps the most obvious set of real-life examples in which people make claims about evil. All of us are familiar with the 9/11 terrorist attacks on the World Trade

Center in New York, in which a group of conspirators, motivated by political animosity towards the United States, flew passenger jets into office buildings and killed thousands of innocent people. Who can forget the images of the planes slamming into the towers, the billowing smoke, the panicked workers fleeing the scene as the falling bodies rained down? If any politically motivated act counts as terrifying, surely this is it. The actions of these terrorists were not ordinary, everyday wrongs. To many shocked observers this seemed to be wrongdoing on another level. It is no surprise that 9/11 prompted extremely strong moral condemnation, and some of those who condemned it chose to use the language of evil. In his State of the Union address in 2002 President George W. Bush declared that 'Evil is real, and it must be opposed.' Going far beyond the 9/11 attacks, Bush also described the nations of Iran, Iraq, and North Korea as an 'axis of evil'. Bush's regular references to evil in the wake of these attacks were contentious at the time and remain so. No doubt this is partly due to the view, common amongst his critics, that Bush was a simplistic thinker, a rigid religious conservative, and a dangerously hawkish president. Critics of Bush's subsequent war on terror might be inclined to reject his use of the language of evil precisely because they see this language as an expression of the mindset that led him to invade Iraq and Afghanistan. On the other side of the political fence, supporters of the President and of the war on terror applauded Bush for condemning the terrorists in the strongest possible terms and for taking a clear and unambiguous moral stand.

The controversy over Bush's statements about 9/11 led to a resurgence of philosophical interest in the topic of evil. Regardless of what we think about President Bush's subsequent policy decisions, philosophers invite us to address some basic moral questions about 9/11. Did the terrorists perform evil actions on that day? Were the terrorists evil people? One possible reason for answering no to both questions is the belief that the so-called terrorists' actions were not even morally wrong, let alone evil.

We might reach this conclusion if we accept the idea that 'One man's terrorist is another man's freedom fighter', and that there is no objective fact as to what is right and what is wrong. If nothing is morally wrong, then it makes no sense to condemn the 9/11 attacks as evil. Another way to support the claim that the terrorists' actions were not wrong would be to claim that US citizens deserved to be attacked and killed as a result of morally corrupt US foreign policy. But, of course, these claims themselves are highly contentious. Many of us think that the 9/11 attackers committed mass murder of innocent civilians, and that their actions were clearly and objectively morally wrong. The challenge that I will focus on comes from philosophers who agree that the 9/11 terrorists' actions were clearly and objectively wrong, but who claim that the terrorists did not do evil. In later chapters of this book we will see in more detail why these philosophers are sceptical about evil and why others disagree. For now, let us hold 9/11 in mind as a key contested example.

Terrorism occurs not only as part of carefully plotted conspiracies, but on a smaller scale as well. Think about Dylann Roof's terrorist attack on churchgoers in Charleston, South Carolina, in 2015. Roof, a white supremacist motivated by a desire to incite a race war between black and white Americans, attended a Bible study meeting at the Emanuel African Methodist Episcopal Church, where he unleashed an attack that was premeditated, politically driven, and fuelled by hatred of his victims. He killed nine innocent people, shooting them at point blank range while they cowered on the floor. Roof acted alone, but, like the 9/11 terrorists, he was ideologically motivated. He falsely believed that his actions were justified, and he craved wide publicity. As his victims lay scattered around him Roof told one of the churchgoers that he would leave her alive so that she could report to the world what he had done, and why he had done it. This, too, is no ordinary case of wrongdoing. Plenty of people used the language of evil to condemn what Roof did that day. A survivor of the attack, Felicia Sanders, said that the church members had welcomed Roof in for

Bible study, and prior to the shooting 'he just sat there the whole time, evil, evil, evil as can be'.

Roof's crime echoes the mass murder committed by the Norwegian terrorist Anders Behring Breivik, who in 2011 set off a bomb that killed nine people, and then travelled to the island of Utøya, where he stalked and murdered sixty-nine children who were on summer camp. Breivik reported that he planned and carried out this massacre because he wanted to draw attention to his anti-leftist and anti-Islamic manifesto. Like Roof, Breivik remained proud and self-righteous. Some commentators, as well as Breivik's defence lawyer, claimed that he was insane and hence not fully responsible for his actions. The chief of domestic intelligence in Norway, Janne Kristiansen, disagreed, saying that Breivik was evil, not insane.

Alongside Roof and Breivik stand a long line of terrorists from around the world who have committed atrocities in the name of their favoured causes. There are the members of the National Thowheeth Jama'ath terrorist group who killed 259 people in the Easter Sunday bombings of churches and hotels in Sri Lanka in 2019. In that same year Brenton Tarrant live-streamed his slaughter of worshippers at mosques in New Zealand. Then there is Salman Ramadan Abedi, the suicide bomber who killed twenty-two concertgoers at the Manchester Arena in 2017. There are the members of the Brussels ISIL terror cell who slaughtered 130 people in Paris in 2015, machine gunning pedestrians and trapping many of their victims in the Bataclan Theatre. There are the ten members of Lashka-e-Taiba who rampaged through Mumbai in 2008, killing at least 164 innocent victims. Finally, we should not forget the terrorist group ranked as the world's most deadly, Nigeria's Boko Haram, who have killed tens of thousands over the previous decade.

These are not cartoon villains. They are not fictional characters from fanciful stories. They are all too real, and too common.

Are these terrorists evildoers? President Bush certainly thinks that they are, and it is worth noting that this is not a judgement that follows partisan political lines. President Barack Obama, for instance, agrees with Bush. When addressing the United Nations in 2014, Obama said of ISIL, 'There can be no reasoning—no negotiation—with this brand of evil.' President Donald Trump has labelled terrorists 'evil losers'. British Prime Minister Tony Blair, in response to the London Bombings in 2005, called on Britons to confront the 'evil ideology' of the terrorists, words echoed a year later by Prime Minister David Cameron, who called for resistance to 'this evil terrorist threat'. What do you think that these politicians mean when they use the language of evil in relation to terrorism? Do you agree with this emphatic condemnation of the actions in question, or do you think that these politicians have made a mistake? If you do think that it is a mistake to condemn the terrorists' actions as evil, what is the nature of that mistake?

Let us move from terrorism to the next set of contested examples, the serial killers. Here, too, options abound. Serial killers are perhaps even more disconcerting than terrorists, given that they kill not in order to achieve some political aim, but for the pleasure that they take in the killing. Descriptions of these cases may seem gratuitous, but in order to morally evaluate them, we must be aware of some of the details. Many serial killers restrain and torture their victims for hours or even days before they kill them, as did the BTK (Bind, Torture, Kill) killer Dennis Rader, and Fred and Rosemary West. Many serial killers end their victims' lives in the process of horrific sexual assault. This sexual motive was present in the cases of Ted Bundy, John Wayne Gacy, and the so-called Butcher of Hanover, Fritz Haarmann, who killed at least twenty-four victims by biting through their throats. Some sadistic killers specifically target young children. Ian Brady and Myra Hindley, for example, raped and killed at least five children in and around Manchester in the 1960s, before burying their bodies on the moors. Most serial killers act secretively, although some, including Rader, the Son of Sam killer David Berkowitz, and the

9

Beltway Snipers, court notoriety by sending taunting letters to police. Many serial killers are recalcitrant, committing atrocities year after year, and continuing even when it is clear that the authorities are closing in.

It is truly sickening to discover the details of the acts committed by serial killers. Many of these crimes are so grisly that we find them not only disgusting, but disorienting, mind-boggling, impossible to understand. People are thus more likely to say that serial killers, as opposed to politically motivated terrorists, are mentally ill rather than evil. This thought is worth examining. If a killer is a psychopath, for instance, does this excuse him from blame? Are psychopaths dangerous, but not morally responsible for what they do, and hence not evil? The short answer is 'Not so fast!' The category of mental illness itself is very broad, and the classification of specific mental illnesses is troublingly vague. Most people who suffer from a mental illness are nonetheless legally and morally responsible for their actions. Moreover, while psychopathic serial killers typically do exhibit some mental deficits in relation to empathy and reasoning skills, it is an exaggeration to say that they are bumbling fools who know not what they do. Many serial killers plan their misdeeds well in advance, understand clearly the fact that they are harming others, and carefully cover their tracks to avoid detection. Serial killers may well be sick, in some sense of that word, but this does not imply that they are excusable. In fact, it is common for journalists and others to use the label 'evil' to describe serial killers and their actions. Ted Bundy's lawyer Polly Nelson said that he was 'the very definition of heartless evil'. Myra Hindley was tagged by the press as 'the most evil woman in Britain'. Do these serial killers and their horrific and seemingly incomprehensible actions constitute the most central examples of evil? Or are we indulging in some kind of unrealistic fantasy when we call them evil?

The crimes committed by sadistic serial killers may be the most intimate and disgusting of all, but for sheer numerical scale of wrongdoing we must turn to the dictators, the war criminals, those who harness the machinery of the military and the state and turn them to mass murder. In our time of increasingly polarized public debate much attention has been paid to Godwin's law. The original formulation of this so-called law reads, 'As an online discussion grows longer, the probability of a comparison involving Hitler approaches 1.' This is more frequently twisted into something like the following form: No matter what the topic under debate, the first person to mention Hitler loses the argument. The idea that this really is a law may be appealing to rhetorical point-scorers longing for a 'Gotcha!' moment, but it cannot survive critical scrutiny. When grappling with the topic of evil, it is intellectually irresponsible *not* to mention Hitler.

The word 'evil' is regularly used to describe the Nazi atrocities. Hitler's militaristic expansionism led directly to the Second World War, in which approximately sixty million people—3 per cent of the world's population—were killed. The amount of destruction and suffering for which Hitler is responsible vastly overshadows that caused by even the most diligent serial killers. Of all of the events in the Second World War it is the Holocaust that draws most attention as a locus of evil. Jews who had lived peacefully alongside their German, Polish, and Hungarian neighbours were systematically stripped of their property, sent to ghettos, packed into railway cattle wagons, and transported to camps where they were worked to death or murdered with poison gas. This was cold-blooded, industrialized genocide. Photographs of the emaciated bodies piled outside the Nazi crematoria reveal a horrific truth, not a fairy-tale or a fantasy. What happened in these camps, these millions upon millions of murders, was morally wrong, but phrasing it in that way seems to understate the case. It was not merely wrong, but evil, or so say some survivors, as well as some scholars who have written about the Holocaust. The political and military leaders who orchestrated this most shameful chapter of human history—Hitler, Himmler, and

Eichmann, amongst others—were not just morally corrupt. It is tempting to say that they were evil.

While the Holocaust seems to be a relatively uncontentious example of evil, complexities arise when we begin morally evaluating specific people who worked within the Nazi system. The historians Christopher Browning and Daniel Goldhagen disagree as to whether the 'ordinary Germans' who participated in the *Einsatzgruppen*—the Nazi death squads—were motivated by anti-Semitic hatred, or bore no malice towards their victims and were merely following orders. This echoes an earlier dispute over Hannah Arendt's claim that the war criminal Adolf Eichmann himself was not a sadistic and anti-Semitic monster but was simply a thoughtless man who wanted to do well at his job. The trial of Eichmann, according to Arendt, reveals the banality of evil. As we shall see in Chapter 4, Arendt almost certainly misread Eichmann's motives and character. Nonetheless, many thinkers have agreed with Arendt's suggestion that some evildoers are sober and obedient bureaucrats, rather than sadistic and wilfully malicious pleasure seekers. Further complex moral questions arise regarding those who were to some degree complicit in the atrocities of the Holocaust. These include the ordinary citizens who knew what was happening and did nothing to help the victims, as well as the concentration camp inmates who assisted in the running of the camps in return for favours from the guards.

Extreme wrongdoing in a time of war raises tough questions about duress, legitimate self-protection, and the cost of moral resistance. Nonetheless, there are plenty of examples from the Holocaust and other atrocities in which perpetrators were not under duress, but actively sought out the opportunity to kill innocent victims in coordinated waves of destruction. In Cambodia in the 1970s the Khmer Rouge abducted, tortured, and murdered anyone who was considered an enemy of the state, including ethnic minorities and 'intellectuals': that is, people with an education, and people who wore glasses. The final death toll in Cambodia is estimated at

1.5 to 3 million. In Rwanda in 1994 a simmering political conflict spilled over into genocide. The Hutu majority rose up and slaughtered up to one million Tutsis in a period of a hundred days. Most of the victims were hacked to death with machetes. Many were killed by their neighbours. Rape was used systematically as a weapon of war. These atrocities are not merely horrific, but overwhelming in scale. Even if we limit ourselves to the 20th century, we can add Stalin and Mao as leaders who are responsible for many millions of deaths. These tyrants and war criminals deserve our strongest condemnation, and this is why they are regularly described as 'evil', a word that Christopher Hitchens described as 'the best negative superlative that we possess'.

We have confronted three kinds of extreme wrongdoing that ordinary people often describe as evil: terrorism, serial killings, and genocidal war crimes. These cases need to be taken seriously. We cannot point to examples of purported evildoing in science fiction, fantasy, or in religious texts, then simply claim that because these things are fictional, there is no evil in the real world. People who are sceptical of the existence of evil must also be willing to point to real acts of terrorism, serial killings, and war crimes, and explain why none of these count as evil. Many of the philosophers who believe that evil exists do not believe in supernatural evil, or, indeed, in the existence of a supernatural realm. Instead, these philosophers think that evil is one example of a moral property. There are many other moral properties, positive or negative, that can be possessed by actions and by people. For example, an action might have the property of being unfair, or generous, or permissible, or blameworthy. A person might have the property of being compassionate, or cruel, or dishonest, or just. When we want to figure out what cruelty is, or what compassion is, rather than launch into grand, unconstrained metaphysical theorizing, we need to examine examples of the kind of things that are typically called cruel, or compassionate. The same goes for evil. (While we are thinking about the importance of focusing on the real world, it is worth pointing out that the vast

13

majority of extreme wrongdoers throughout history have been men. In order to reflect this, I will predominately use male pronouns when referring to someone who is judged to be an evildoer. This is not intended to imply that all evildoers are men.)

By shifting our focus from fictional cases to the most confronting real-life examples of wrongdoing, we raise the stakes in the debate about evil. But this shift does not in itself settle the question of whether evil exists, nor the question of what evil is supposed to be. Suppose that we do point at real instances of terrorism or serial killing and denounce them as evil. What is it that we are saying about them? Are we saying that they are morally wrong? That they are very wrong? Do they have some special feature in common that distinguishes them from ordinary, non-evil wrongs? If so, which feature? Do evil actions, unlike ordinary wrongs, have a distinctive kind of effect on their victims? Do evil actions, unlike ordinary wrongs, induce a certain kind of reaction—perhaps horror, or incomprehension—from onlookers? Do evil actions, unlike ordinary wrongs, come from a distinctive kind of motive? We must also answer a parallel set of questions about evil people. It is all well and good to point at Hitler and Ted Bundy and say 'They are evil', but if we condemn them in this way, what is it that we are saying about them? What do evil people have in common that distinguishes them from ordinary, non-evil people? Does an evil person have a radically different psychological profile compared to the rest of us? Are evil people born evil? Can evil people be fixed?

These are the questions that philosophers must address when we set out an account of evil. Even amongst the philosophers who think that evil exists, there is much disagreement over exactly what evil is supposed to be, and over where the boundary line of evil lies. We have seen that the central *prima facie* cases of evil include terrorism, serial killing, and genocidal war crimes. Each of these central cases has all of the following key features: the acts in question are morally wrong; the wrongdoers are culpable or blameworthy for what they have done; these were acts of intentional killing or torture; and in each case there were numerous innocent victims.

When it comes to identifying the boundary between the evil and the merely bad, it is important not merely to focus on the central cases, but to compare these to a variety of more peripheral or problematic examples, and finally to compare them to actions and people that clearly fall short of being evil. We can explore the periphery by considering instances of severe wrongdoing which lack one or more of the key features possessed by the central cases. For example, in the central cases the perpetrators are obviously blameworthy for their actions, but sometimes the culpability of people who inflict extreme harm on others is not so straightforward. The murder of the toddler James Bulger by two 10-year-olds, Robert Thompson and Jon Venables, provides one tragic illustration of this kind of case. While the killers were called evil by many in the press, others rejected this label, claiming that Thompson and Venables were mere children themselves, and hence not properly responsible for what they had done. Opinion is similarly divided over Lynndie England, the US soldier who participated in the torture and humiliation of Iraqi prisoners at Abu Ghraib prison. Some people see England as a clear example of an evildoer, but others think that she was coerced by the ringleader of the torturers, Charles Graner, and hence was less than fully responsible for her actions.

We can generate more peripheral cases by focusing on other features that were present in the core examples. In the central *prima facie* cases of evil the perpetrators torture or kill *innocent* victims, but we can imagine possible peripheral cases in which the perpetrators inflict this kind of extreme suffering only on guilty parties. For example, consider the gleefully sadistic executioner, who kills only those who (let us say, for the sake of argument) have rightly been sentenced to death. He takes great pleasure in snuffing out their lives, but does he do evil? Or think about the

Red Army soldiers who brutalized enemy combatants as they drove the German troops out of the Motherland. Given that the Germans had invaded first and had already committed many atrocities of their own, arguably the German soldiers were not innocent victims. Does this imply that the Russians did not commit evil when they tortured and executed them?

In the central *prima facie* cases of evil, perpetrators not only *intend* to inflict extreme harm, they succeed in doing so. What should we say about people who intend and attempt to inflict carnage on innocent victims, but are thwarted by bad luck or by the authorities, and end up harming no one? Think about the so-called shoe bomber, Richard Reid, who tried but failed to bring down a trans-Atlantic flight in 2001. Reid's failed attempt seems to be an extremely wrong action, but was it evil? Did Reid fall short of doing evil simply because luck did not go his way? Another challenging peripheral case is that of the sadistic voyeur, who inflicts no harm herself, but who secretly takes great pleasure in watching the extreme suffering of innocent people, such as those dying in natural disasters. Her actions seem to be morally repulsive, but they are harmless actions nonetheless. Can a harmless action count as evil? A final set of possible peripheral cases are those in which the harms inflicted by the perpetrator do not consist of torture or killing, but nonetheless are extreme. Consider the horrendous child sexual abuse carried out by priests in the Catholic Church. Think of Josef Fritzl, who imprisoned his own daughter in the basement for twenty-four years, raping her repeatedly. These are terrible wrongs, and many people would describe them as evil. But what about a single act of rape, or an isolated case of torture? It is unclear how far down the scale of extremity we have to go before that label 'evil' seems inappropriate. Similar questions of scale occur in relation to the number of victims. Each of the *prima facie* central cases of evildoers that we considered earlier—terrorists, serial killers, and war criminals—has numerous victims. If there is only one victim rather than many, can an action still count as evil?

These are the kinds of questions that we will be exploring in Chapters 2–6. It should be obvious by now that this is difficult territory: not merely intellectually complex and confusing, but morally disturbing. The domain of moral extremity evokes powerful emotions, produces strong disagreements, and elicits many vague and confusing pronouncements. In what follows I will introduce you to some of the most interesting disagreements amongst philosophers who have offered accounts of evil. We will explore the various ways in which philosophers have tried to distinguish that which is evil from that which is merely bad or wrong. By the end of this book hopefully you will have a clearer idea of what evil is supposed to be, and thus will be in a better position to judge whether there are any evil actions and any evil people in the real world. No doubt some of you will remain sceptical about the existence of evil. Either way, in the process you should acquire a deeper understanding of extreme wrongdoing and human depravity, in all of its awful variety.

Chapter 2
The horror and incomprehensibility of evil action

On Easter Sunday in 2019 terrorists from the National Thowheeth Jama'ath group detonated a series of bombs in churches and hotels in Sri Lanka, killing 259 people. In response to this event the US politician Elizabeth Warren tweeted, 'To slaughter worshippers at church during Easter service is an act of great evil.' What did Warren intend to convey by this? Why didn't she just say that this kind of mass killing is wrong? Warren chose the language of evil in order to condemn the bombings in the strongest possible terms. Evil is not ordinary, or humdrum, or unremarkable. Evil is *different*. Evil is *distinctive*. But how, exactly, are evil actions different? Are there special features possessed by evil actions that mark them out from the class of ordinary, non-evil actions? Philosophers have offered a range of answers to these questions, and we will now begin to engage with their competing accounts of evil in more detail. A good philosophical account of evil action will consist in a definition of evil action that is both true and explanatory: a definition that accurately describes the nature of evil actions, and allows us to see how they differ from actions that are not evil. We should reject any definition that is too broad, that mistakenly includes things that are not really evil actions. Equally, we should reject any definition that is too narrow, that mistakenly excludes things that really are evil actions.

The first step in building a plausible definition of evil action is to get clear on the relationship between evil and wrong. When we think about Warren's choice of the word 'evil' in her denunciatory tweet, it seems obvious that calling an action evil is not *equivalent* to calling it wrong. Even though they are not equivalent, there does seem to be some overlap between the concepts of evil and wrong. Consider an analogy: calling someone a mother is not equivalent to calling someone a parent, but that does not imply that the category of mother does not overlap with the category of parent. As we all know, being a mother is one way of being a parent, but not the only way of being a parent. The class of mothers is a subclass within the broader class of parents. Every mother is a parent, but not every parent is a mother. It seems likely that this mirrors the relationship between evil actions and wrong actions. Elizabeth Warren did not explicitly say that the terrorist bombings were wrong, but when she said that they were evil actions she implied that they were also wrong. If an action is evil, then it must also be impermissible: the kind of thing that we ought not to do. Imagine how baffling it would have been if Warren had said that the terrorists' actions were evil, but then added that what they did was OK, or was well justified. When Warren called their actions evil, she was implicitly telling us that they are morally wrong actions. Every evil action is also a wrong action. Not every wrong action is evil, though. When we consider a broad range of examples, plenty of wrongs seem to fall short of being evil. Shoplifting, for example, is morally wrong, but it is not evil. Lying about your age in order to get into a nightclub is morally wrong, but not evil. The reason that these wrong actions fail to count as evil is that they are minor, even trivial. These minor wrongs are not terrible, awful, or appalling. In contrast, evil actions are terrible, awful, and appalling. Evil actions have a moral gravity. They are significant. They must be taken seriously. Warren chose to use the label 'evil' because she was trying to convey this sense of moral gravity.

This pushes us towards a very basic philosophical account of evil action. When a terrorist blows up a roomful of innocent people, he has done something that is *much worse* than shoplifting or lying. Perhaps the best definition of evil actions is that they are simply extremely wrong actions, or actions that are much worse than ordinary, everyday wrongs. The concept of evil action, on this account, picks out the red zone at the extreme end of the spectrum of wrongdoing. Evil action is nothing more than very wrong action.

The basic extremity account of evil action: An action is evil if and only if it is extremely wrong.

This definition of evil action is attractive in its simplicity, and it appears to fit nicely with many common judgements as to which specific actions are evil. It would allow us to explain why torture and mass murder are evil. They are evil simply because they are extremely wrong. The basic extremity account would also allow us to explain why shoplifting is wrong but not evil. Shoplifting falls short of being evil because it is not extreme. But things cannot be settled so quickly when we are thinking philosophically! Let us consider a complication that arises within the basic extremity account, and then some objections to this way of thinking about evil.

The complication arises when we ask what it means for one action to be more wrong than another, or when we ask in which respect evil actions are extreme. After all, there are many distinct dimensions along which we could rank wrong actions. Some wrong actions inflict a greater amount of harm than others. Some wrong actions have a greater number of victims than others. Some wrong actions were performed from more deplorable motives than others. Some wrong actions are more horrific than others. Some wrong actions are more worthy of prevention than others. Moreover, we have no reason to believe that all of these various kinds of extremity will neatly stick together.

Instead, it seems that they will come apart. Action A might be more harmful than action B, even though action B was performed from worse motives than those that lay behind action A. Action A might be more worthy of prevention than action B, even though action B is more horrific than action A. If we do claim that evil actions, by definition, are extreme moral wrongs, then we will need to specify which of these various kinds of extremity we are talking about. This is no easy task.

Suppose for a moment that we take the relevant factor to be the amount of harm that is inflicted by the wrong action. According to this view, evil actions ought to be defined as *extremely harmful* wrong actions.

The extremely harmful wrongs account of evil action: An action is evil if and only if it is an extremely harmful wrong.

This view has its advocates, but it has also attracted much criticism. The first objection to the extremely harmful wrongs account is as follows: if evil is nothing more than extremely harmful wrongdoing, then how could we explain the fact that so many people are sceptical about the existence of evil? Scepticism about evil would make more sense if evil was supposed to be something more complex and more contentious than merely extremely harmful wrongdoing. A second objection to the extremely harmful wrongs account is popular amongst philosophers who have written on this topic over the past few decades. Some of these philosophers claim that evil is not merely quantitatively different from ordinary wrongdoing, but is qualitatively different. They believe that evil actions are not simply *more* wrong or *more harmful* than ordinary non-evil wrongs, and hence they reject the extremely harmful wrongs account of evil action. They propose instead that we define evil actions by identifying the extra quality or property that they possess, a property that is entirely lacking in ordinary, non-evil wrongs.

Why have these philosophers endorsed the view that evil actions are qualitatively different from ordinary wrongs? One reason is their desire to draw a sharp line between the two categories of evil and non-evil, ruling out the possibility of cases that are a little bit evil, somewhat evil, or kind of evil. If there is a qualitative rather than quantitative difference here then the difference between evil and non-evil will be a matter of black and white, and never shades of grey. This fits nicely with the fact that people who condemn an action as evil seem to be making an emphatic judgement. There is another quite different reason why many of these philosophers think that evil is qualitatively different from ordinary wrongs. They are responding to a sceptical challenge from critics who think that there is no such thing as evil, and that we should simply drop the concept. The defenders of the concept of evil believe that it will be easier to rebuff this sceptical challenge if they can show that evil action is radically different from ordinary wrongdoing. If 'evil action' were taken to mean 'very wrong action', then it seems that we would simply be able to replace our talk of evil with talk of extreme wrongness, and nothing significant would be lost. Yet these philosophers think that our talk about evil is distinctive and important, and worth preserving rather than replacing. They believe that the best way to defend the concept of evil against the threat of erasure is to show that evil actions are qualitatively distinct from ordinary wrongs.

Ultimately I am not convinced that there is a qualitative rather than quantitative difference between evil actions and ordinary wrongs, but I must confess that most of the philosophers who have addressed this issue disagree with me. The view held by my opponents is worth exploring in detail. These philosophers reject the basic extremity account of evil actions, claiming instead that evil actions contain some distinctive extra ingredient, not merely more of the badness that is present in ordinary wrongs. There are several places that we could look when trying to locate this posited qualitative difference: in the reactions of victims and third-party observers, or in the psychology of the people who perform the actions, or in the nature of the harms inflicted by the actions. In the remainder of this chapter we will explore the possibility that evil actions stand out from ordinary wrongs insofar as they elicit a qualitatively distinct kind of reaction from victims or from observers, and we will move on to assess the other options in Chapters 3 and 4.

Could it be that evil actions count as evil because of the distinctive way that they make us feel? At first glance, this approach might appear to be alarmingly subjective. Philosophy is supposed to be about getting at reality, not putting feelings before facts. Yet it is not outlandish to suggest that evil actions might be defined according to how they make us feel. Some very familiar and perfectly respectable concepts are designed to pick out groups of things in virtue of the reactions that those things cause in us. Think, for example, about the category of the funny. All sorts of disparate things count as funny: a witty joke, a clumsy stumble, an accidental misspelling, an exaggerated facial expression, a child's mispronunciation of a word. If we go searching for the objective and independent property that all of these things have in common, chances are we will come up empty-handed. But this doesn't show that nothing counts as funny, nor that there is something wrong with the concept of the funny. Things count as funny because they are apt to amuse us, and this helps to explain the fact that so many wildly varied things all count as funny.

Philosophers sometimes use the label 'response-dependent' to refer to properties that are defined in terms of our reactions. The proposal at hand is that evil, like funny, is a response-dependent property. Actions count as evil because of the way that they make us feel, and it is this distinctive phenomenology that distinguishes evil from everyday wrongdoing, or so this story goes. But which specific responses or reactions are plausible candidates? To help answer this question, ask yourself how *you* feel when contemplating paradigmatic cases of evil action. How do you feel when watching a documentary detailing Ted Bundy's abduction, torture, and murder of a stream of young women? What emotions well up in you when you look at the famous cross-sectional diagrams of slave transport ships, with the living bodies stacked head to toe? How do you react when you watch film footage of the gas chambers at Auschwitz, the piles of corpses, the pain in the eyes of the emaciated survivors? In response to these extreme wrongs many of us recoil in horror. Some people report similar emotional reactions: being chilled, disgusted, appalled, sickened, aghast. For the sake of simplicity, let us use the word 'horrified' as a label for this group of emotional reactions.

The idea that there is a connection between evil and horror seems promising. But what is the nature of this connection? Can we define evil action in terms of its connection to feelings of horror? First let us consider a very simple version of a response-dependent account of evil action.

The horrifying account of evil action: An action is evil if and only if it causes feelings of horror.

This account does fit with some of the key examples that we have considered. Lots of *prima facie* evil actions induce horror in observers, including the Sri Lankan terrorist attacks condemned by Elizabeth Warren. In contrast, minor wrongs like shoplifting often induce moral disapproval, even indignation, but not horror. Unfortunately, though, the horrifying account quickly runs into significant problems. Plenty of actions that are horrifying, sickening, or disgusting are not evil. For example, watching someone walk a tightrope across a chasm induces gut-wrenching horror in many observers. Yet no one thinks that it is evil to undertake such daring feats, sickening as they might be. (The daredevil Evel Knievel got his nickname from his surname, not from his death-defying motorcycle jumps.) Many actions that induce feelings of disgust—swallowing raw fish guts, or cleaning out a portable toilet—are not evil either. But perhaps we are being unfair to the advocates of this kind of response-dependent account of evil. They could claim that there are different kinds of horror, and different kinds of disgust. If the kind of horror or disgust that is induced by contact with fish guts does not feel the same as the distinctly moral kind of horror or disgust that is induced by contemplating the actions of a serial killer, then we might be able to defend the claim that evil actions are distinguished from ordinary wrongs in virtue of inducing a distinctive feeling. This allows us to put forward a revised version of the response-dependent account.

The morally horrifying account of evil action: An action is evil if and only if it causes feelings of moral horror.

This definition of evil action is more attractive than its predecessor. On this account torture and genocide are evil because they induce moral horror, whereas shoplifting is not evil because it does not induce horror at all, and eating raw fish guts is not evil because it induces mere non-moral horror, mere gross-out disgust.

Despite this improvement the morally horrifying account of evil action still faces a significant objection. Imagine that you are studying at film school and you are required to make a short film as your final assessment task. You decide to make a documentary about the 1994 Rwandan genocide, detailing the shocking violence, and examining the way in which survivors and perpetrators have managed to live side by side in the years since the atrocity. Given your skill as a budding film-maker, when you screen your work for your classmates they are repeatedly moved to feel moral horror and disgust. In screening this film you have now done something that induced moral horror in observers. According to the morally horrifying account of evil action, this is exactly what it takes for an action to count as evil. So much the worse for this definition of evil action, we might say. Your screening of this documentary did cause feelings of moral horror, but your action was not even morally wrong, let alone evil. Thus it cannot be the case that evil actions are those actions which cause feelings of moral horror.

Something seems a little bit odd about this objection, though. Let us step back for a minute to consider an important distinction that holds true for all emotions. This is the distinction between the cause of an emotion and what philosophers call the intentional object of that emotion. The intentional object of an emotion is the thing that the emotion is directed at, the thing that it is *about*. It can be difficult to notice this distinction, because often the thing that causes you to feel an emotion is identical to the thing the emotion is directed at. For example, if a snake slithers out in front of you, the snake causes you to be afraid, and it is the snake that you are afraid of. In some cases, though, the cause of an emotion is not identical with the intentional object of that emotion. You might cause me to become afraid by telling me about the risks that come with future global warming. Here my fear was caused by your words, but I am not afraid of your words. My fear is directed at something else: namely, the future global warming. To put it in more ordinary terms, what caused me to be afraid need not be identical with what I am afraid of.

Keeping in mind this distinction between the cause of an emotion and the intentional object of that emotion, let us return to the case of the morally horrifying documentary about genocide. The emotions of moral horror and moral disgust experienced by the audience are caused by your actions as the film-maker, but their emotions are not directed at your actions. The audience are horrified by the slaughter carried out by the Hutus, not by your screening of the film. This suggests a way in which we could refine our response-dependent account of evil action so that it will not be vulnerable to the previous objection. Perhaps evil actions are not those that cause moral horror, but those at which we direct moral horror, those which are the intentional object of moral horror.

> **The directed morally horrifying account of evil action**:
> An action is evil if and only if it is an action at which we direct feelings of moral horror.

Again, this account is an improvement on its predecessor, but it remains vulnerable to some powerful challenges. Who is the 'we' in this definition of evil action? Not everyone is horrified by the same things. Some people have a dulled capacity for emotional responses. They might look upon the most extreme kind of wrongdoing without batting an eyelid, especially if the wrongdoing in question was not noticeably gory or viscerally disgusting. The converse is also possible. Some people have oversensitive and misaligned emotional responses. They might feel genuine moral horror when confronted with actions that are not even morally wrong. Think, for example, about homosexual behaviour. (For the sake of argument let us agree that homosexual acts are morally permissible. There is nothing morally wrong about living a gay or lesbian life. People who disagree on this issue can choose a different example.) Although homosexual acts are not morally wrong, there are communities in which the majority of people feel not mere disapproval, but moral horror and disgust towards homosexual behaviour. If the directed morally horrifying account of evil action were correct, this would imply that homosexual acts *are* evil, because this account says that acts that are the object of moral horror are evil. But it is not plausible in this case to say that homosexual behaviour is evil, because it is not even morally wrong! The underlying problem is that moral emotions can misfire. Sometimes the moral emotions of entire communities can misfire, due to prejudice or other kinds of false belief. What actually morally horrifies some people is not likely to correspond with what really is the most egregious, awful, and extreme wrongdoing.

Things are not looking good for response-dependent accounts of evil action. The idea that evil can be characterized by its distinctive feel seems to be undermined by the fact that often different people feel very different things in relation to one and the same action, and that some of these feelings are misguided and unjustified. The philosopher Marcus Singer thinks that we can solve this problem by slightly tweaking the response-dependent account. Singer claims that evil actions should be defined as the kind of action at which people *should* direct moral horror. This move is roughly equivalent to taking the 'we' in the previous definition of evil action to mean something like 'wise and good people who are fully aware of all of the relevant facts, and who have well-attuned moral emotions'. This group of people will feel morally horrified by all and only the things that genuinely justify feelings of horror, by what we might call the 'horrorworthy wrongs'.

After all of these modifications we have ended up with a definition that looks to be significantly more plausible.

> **The horrorworthy account of evil action:** An action is evil if and only if it is a worthy object of moral horror.

This definition of evil action seems to be accurate. It allows us to distinguish genuinely evil actions from actions that are merely gross, revolting, or terrifying in non-moral ways. The horrorworthy account also suggests that torture and genocide are evil, because good and wise people *would* be horrified when they contemplate these heinous wrongs. This definition also fits with the view that shoplifting is not evil. If any actual feelings of moral horror did happen to be directed at a minor wrong like shoplifting, those feelings could be dismissed as being disproportionate, and hence not indicative of what is evil. The fact that some groups of people are morally horrified by homosexual behaviour would not create a problem for this kind of definition, so long as these groups do not count as wise and good people who have well-attuned moral emotions. All in all, the horrorworthy account of evil action looks to be pretty convincing. There is only one problem. This definition does not have the right kind of explanatory power to function as a good philosophical account of evil action.

Consider the following analogy. Imagine that you want to understand what makes an action count as admirably courageous.

You take into account factors such as the amount of danger that is involved in carrying out the action, the degree to which the action is self-interested or altruistic, the kind of knowledge that the agent has about the risk involved, and the rightness or wrongness of the action. These are all considerations that strike you as things that might make an action more or less admirably courageous. But then suppose that your friend suggests an alternative answer to your question. Why not just say that an admirably courageous action, by definition, is the kind of action that deserves to be praised and admired as brave, the kind of action that good and well-informed people would actually admire as brave? This claim is true, for what it is worth, but it is not a helpful answer to your question. Your friend has put the cart before the horse. The problem with your friend's definition is that it is silent on the question of which features make an action worthy of this kind of admiration. It does not tell you why some actions deserve this kind of admiration while others do not. It does not have any explanatory power.

With this analogy in hand, let us reconsider the horrorworthy account of evil action. Recall that the appeal to moral horror was initially offered as an alternative to the basic view that evil actions are, by definition, extremely wrong actions. The distinctive feel of moral horror was supposed to constitute a qualitative difference between evils and ordinary wrongs. But now we are considering the view that evil actions, by definition, are those that *ought to* give rise to this distinctive feeling, actions that are *worthy of* moral horror. What does it take for an action to be a worthy object of moral horror? The answer, it seems, is that the action must actually be morally wrong, and must be wrong enough to warrant not mere mild disapproval or medium-strength indignation, but full-strength moral horror or disgust. In other words, what makes an action worthy of moral horror is the fact that it is extremely morally wrong. Anyone who tries to explain the nature of evil action by pointing to the horrorworthy account of evil would then have to explain what makes something worthy of horror. In doing so, it would be tempting for them to fall back on something like the basic extremity account, which was the very thing that the response-dependent approach was designed to replace. Elizabeth Warren condemned the Easter Sunday terrorist attacks as evil, and it is true that those attacks are worthy of moral horror. But we cannot explain why these actions count as evil by pointing out that they are worthy of moral horror. Rather, the fact that these actions are worthy of moral horror is explained by the fact that they are extremely wrong, that the perpetrators killed hundreds of innocent victims for no good reason.

I have tried to develop the most convincing version of a response-dependent account of evil, where the response in question consists of feelings of moral horror or moral disgust. In order to be plausible such accounts need to be refined and modified to the point at which they cease to be explanatorily useful, or so I have argued. But what if I began this process by choosing the wrong response on which to build such an account? Some philosophers have suggested that the characteristic response to evil actions is an intellectual rather than emotional response. Many people say that they find evil actions utterly baffling, disorienting, beyond explanation: in a word, *incomprehensible*. Some crimes, such as revenge killings, are undeniably terrible, but they are easy enough to understand. In contrast, the fact that English doctor and serial killer Harold Shipman gave lethal injections to 250 of his patients makes no sense at all. Perhaps the distinction between evil actions and non-evil wrongs is that evils are incomprehensible, whereas ordinary wrongs can be understood. There is a sharp dividing line between that which is incomprehensible and that which can be understood to some degree, so this option might appeal to those philosophers who believe that evil actions are not merely more wrong than ordinary wrongs, but contain an extra quality that is not present in ordinary wrongs to any degree. So, should we define evil actions in terms of incomprehensibility?

The initial challenge is to figure out exactly how to interpret the word 'incomprehensible' in this context. Something is incomprehensible if we cannot understand it, but there are several quite distinct ways in which we could fail to understand an action. The first is not understanding what has been done, in the sense of being unable to recognize, categorize, or interpret the action in question. For example, if you are watching a foreign sport and the referee makes an unfamiliar hand gesture, you might say that the referee's action is incomprehensible. You have no idea what it was that the referee just did. Clearly this cannot be the meaning that is in play in the claim that evil actions are incomprehensible. Shipman's serial murders are *murders*, they are intentional killings of innocent people who do not want to die. Someone who claims to find Shipman's deeds incomprehensible does not mean that she does not know what kind of action he performed. It is more likely that she means she cannot understand *why* Shipman did it. And it is true that it is very difficult to identify the motives that lie behind some *prima facie* evil actions, including Shipman's. Similarly, you might struggle to understand why the Hutus would turn on their Tutsi neighbours and cut them down with machetes. What were they thinking? What were they hoping to achieve? What moved them to act in this way? It might be suggested that the distinctive quality of evil actions, as opposed to ordinary wrongs, is that we cannot identify the motives that lie behind evil actions, and hence that they strike us as baffling.

The unfathomable motive account of evil action: An action is evil if and only if the motives from which it is performed cannot be identified.

While it is true that some evil actions are incomprehensible in this sense, it is not plausible that this counts as the distinctive hallmark of evil action. One obvious problem is that there are plenty of impulsive irrational actions that are completely unfathomable in this sense, but that are not even morally wrong. Imagine that your friend suddenly bends down and starts eating the grass in the yard, and that you are unable to identify the motives from which she is acting. Even though this action is unfathomable, we are not at all inclined to call it evil. It is just harmless, puzzling, and weird. But even if we limit our focus to unfathomable actions that are also significant moral wrongs, it is a mistake to think that all evil actions come from unknown motives. Many prime examples of evil action were performed from motives that we can identify. Indeed, many evildoers tell us explicitly why they did what they did. Terrorists and ideologically motivated war criminals often broadcast their aims as part of the recruitment process, but the fact that we can identify their motives does nothing to reduce the severity of their wrongdoing, nor to make it less abhorrent. Many serial killers reveal their motives after the fact. We know that John Wayne Gacy, for instance, was moved to torture and kill his victims because he got an intense sexual thrill from doing so, and we know this because he explained this motive in his confession, and because what he said there fits with the accounts of survivors. But imagine how odd it would be for someone to say 'Gacy's actions initially seemed incomprehensible and evil to me. But now I understand that he tortured and murdered those boys because he took intense sexual pleasure in their suffering, so I no longer think that what he did was evil.' Many motives are awful, horrendous, malicious, and worthy of the strongest condemnation. Grasping those motives does not and should not lead us to moderate our condemnation of the actions in question.

However, there is another possible interpretation of the claim that evil actions are, by definition, incomprehensible wrongs. When people say that an evil action is an incomprehensible wrong, maybe they mean something like 'This action is wrong, and I can't imagine ever choosing to do something like that myself.' This gives rise to another possible account of evil action.

The unimaginable wrongs account of evil action:　An action is evil if and only if it is morally wrong, and we cannot imagine choosing to perform that action ourselves.

This is starting to look more like a plausible definition of evil action. Perhaps you can imagine yourself choosing to shoplift and commit other ordinary wrongs, at least in some circumstances. In contrast (I hope!) you cannot imagine ever choosing to strap on a suicide bomber's vest, walk into a church in Sri Lanka on Easter Sunday, and kill hundreds of innocent worshippers. Even though you know what motivated the National Thowheeth Jama'ath terrorists to carry out these bombings, their actions remain incomprehensible to you in this new sense, and hence, according to the account under consideration, their actions would qualify as evil.

Is the difference between evils and ordinary wrongs the fact that we respond to evil actions with this kind of incomprehension? Some alarm bells should be ringing, given our earlier investigation of horror-based response-dependent accounts. Again, we must ask who is the 'we' in this definition. The Sri Lankan terrorists themselves clearly *could* imagine choosing to perform such actions, as can many of their extremist supporters. If incomprehensibility is supposed to be the distinctive hallmark of evil action, then it must be incomprehensibility to the right group of people: namely, the morally good, wise, and well-informed people whose imaginations are a reliable reflection of the moral facts. The evil actions are ones that we *should* never choose to do, and that the good and wise people cannot imagine themselves choosing to do. But if this is the case, we need to ask why the good and wise people would find these particular actions incomprehensible. And surely the answer in the case of evil actions is that they should never be chosen under any circumstances because they are extreme wrongs, or because they would inflict terrible harms on innocent victims. We cannot explain why an action counts as evil by pointing to the fact that a morally good person would never imagine choosing to do it, because the explanation actually runs in the other direction. A morally good person would never imagine herself choosing to perform this action because this action is much worse than ordinary wrongs.

In this chapter we've explored the possibility that the qualitative difference that marks out evil actions is a distinctive response from victims or third-party observers. Similar problems arise for response-dependent accounts regardless of whether we select an emotional response such as moral horror, or an intellectual response such as incomprehension. There does seems to be a connection between evil actions and some kinds of negative response from observers, but it is the extreme wrongness of the actions that determines when horror and incomprehension are appropriate responses, rather than the presence of horror or incomprehension that makes it a fact that the action is extremely wrong. In light of this, we ought to conclude that evil is not really a response-dependent property. You might recall my suggestion that another familiar concept—the funny—does pick out a response-dependent property. What is the difference between the property of being funny and the property of being evil? Most of us are happy to accept the idea that what is funny is determined by what people actually find amusing. If people are amused by your little brother mispronouncing a word, then that is funny. The fact that people are amused by it is what *makes* it qualify as funny. But, of course, some people might not find it amusing, and this is fine. It is easy to be a relativist about the funny. There is what is funny-to-me, and what is funny-to-you, but it is not the case that only one of us is getting things right. People can't get it wrong when it comes to what is funny. In contrast, people can get it wrong when it comes to judging that something is evil, and when it comes to responding properly to evil actions. Some people fail to feel horror towards what really is horrorworthy. Some people, including the National Thowheeth Jama'ath terrorists, can not only imagine choosing to do evil, they actually go ahead and do it. If we want to understand the difference between evil actions and ordinary wrongs, we need to look beyond our reactions.

Chapter 3
The psychological hallmark of evil action

Some people think that we would be better off ditching the concept of evil. They think that evil is nothing more than a myth, and a dangerous one at that. Those of us who want to defend this concept are required to give a plausible and informative definition of evil, and to show that this definition accurately describes some things in the real world. We have seen that some philosophers think that the best way to respond to the sceptical challenge is to claim that evil action is qualitatively distinct from ordinary wrongdoing, and then to identify *which* special quality marks it out. There are three places we could look for such a quality: in our reactions to evil, in the psychology of the evildoer, or in the nature of the harms caused by evil action. In Chapter 2 we saw just how difficult it is to build a convincing response-dependent account that defines evil in terms of our reactions. Now we will move on to consider the possibility that there is a psychological hallmark of evil. This is the view that the difference between evils and ordinary wrongs lies in something distinctive about the motives or the emotional state of the person who performs the evil action.

Does an action count as evil because of some fact about the mind of the evildoer? Think about the actions performed by the terrorist Brenton Tarrant. In 2019 he live-streamed his mass murder of worshippers in two mosques in Christchurch, New Zealand. This strikes many of us as a paradigmatic example of an evil action, but what is the relevant difference between Tarrant's actions and the countless ordinary wrongs that occur every day? Perhaps what makes Tarrant's actions evil is the fact that he acted from a kind of motive that is absent in everyday wrongdoing, or because when Tarrant carried out these murders he felt emotions that are absent in cases of everyday wrongdoing. Something like this view of evil action was put forward by Hannah Arendt in her 1951 book *The Origins of Totalitarianism*. Here she claimed that the industrialized mass slaughter of the Holocaust revealed a 'radical evil' that simply could not be explained by the ordinary motives of 'self-interest, greed, covetousness, resentment, lust for power, and cowardice'. (As we shall see, this is a view that Arendt later disavowed.)

This psychologically focused way of characterizing evil action is worth exploring in detail, but let's step back from thinking about evil and take a moment to consider how we define some other kinds of action. Some kinds of action are *not* defined via reference to the psychology of the agent (that is, the person who performs the action). Think about what it takes for something to count as a harmful action. An action is harmful if and only if it causes harm to someone or something, and actions that cause harm can come from any motive whatsoever, and can be accompanied by any emotion in the agent. Some harmful actions are vindictive, in which case the agent intends to harm the victim. Some harmful actions are not intended by the agent to be harmful, but the agent knowingly inflicts that harm on the victim as a foreseen side-effect of achieving some other desired goal. Some harmful actions are performed out of good intentions and a desire to benefit those who actually end up being harmed. So, a harmful action counts as such purely in virtue of its effects, and not at all in virtue of the psychology of the agent who performs the action. In contrast, many other categories of action *are* defined via reference to the psychology of the agent. What it is for an action to count as compassionate, for example, is for the agent to have acted out of concern for the suffering of another. Some actions that are beneficial in terms of their effects are not compassionate actions, because they did not come from the specific psychological states that are required for an action to be compassionate. Vengeful actions, like compassionate actions, are defined in terms of the psychology of the agent. An action counts as vengeful only if it is performed out of a desire to pay back, to exact revenge, and perhaps if it is accompanied by a kind of anger or ill will towards its victim.

Our aim in this chapter is to figure out whether the category of evil action, like compassionate action and vengeful action, must be defined with reference to the motives or feelings of the agent who performs the action, or whether evil actions, like harmful actions, can come from any motives whatsoever. We also need to consider whether the distinctive psychology of evildoing could be sufficient on its own to distinguish evil from non-evil actions, or whether it might be merely one of the necessary ingredients for evil. Several contemporary philosophers have claimed that evil actions are distinguished from ordinary wrongs in virtue of the psychological state of the evildoer. As we shall see, though, they do not agree with each other as to *which* psychological state is the distinctive source of evil action. We will work through four candidates for the psychological hallmark of evil: malice, sadistic pleasure, knowing defiance, and deliberative silencing.

Let us begin by trying to understand the nature of malice. Suppose that you have a rival in your friendship group who ridicules you in front of your friends. If you feel malice towards her, that means you have hostile feelings towards her, and you want bad things to happen to her. An action counts as malicious if it is an expression of these feelings or desires. If your hostile feelings lead you to hurt or humiliate your rival, you have acted maliciously. We need to think carefully here, because there are some unusual cases in which you might intentionally inflict harm on someone without acting out of malice. For example, suppose that you are trying to teach your beloved younger sister not to harass the dog, because you are worried that the dog, if provoked, is likely to bite her. Suppose further that your sister has not responded to your gentle warnings, nor to your descriptions of the damage that the dog might do, and you come to believe that the only way your sister will learn not to provoke the dog is if the dog gives her a fright. So you intervene, and cause the dog to turn and bark aggressively at your sister. When you see that your sister is distressed you are pleased by this fact. This is what you wanted. But you have not acted maliciously towards your sister in this case. You wanted to make her suffer only as a means to making her safe in the long run. When an act is malicious, the agent wants the victim to suffer not merely as a means to producing some other outcome that is good for the victim. Rather, the malicious agent simply wants the victim to suffer, or wants harm to come to the victim for its own sake. Malice involves feeling ill will towards others, and malicious actions are expressions of this ill will.

Many wrong actions are not malicious. Consider a driver who is on the phone and not paying attention to the road, and who loses control of her car and hits a pedestrian. This is a morally wrong action for which the driver is culpable, but it was due to negligence, not ill will. It certainly was not the case that the driver bore malice towards the pedestrian, a person she had never met, a person she knew nothing about, a person whom she was not thinking about at the time of the incident. In some other situations people deliberately inflict harm on innocent victims, and do so wrongfully, even though they bear no ill will towards those whom they harm. Car thieves typically do not want their victims to suffer. They just want the car! They steal while knowing that they are taking someone else's property, but while bearing no ill will towards the people whom they wrong. (It seems to be true that they show disrespect to the cars' owners, and perhaps that they do not have enough goodwill towards them, but neither of these things amounts to malice.) Similarly, many kinds of wrongdoing that are common in the corporate world—fraud, the selling of fake 'cures', environmental contamination—are motivated by simple greed, rather than by a desire that the victims suffer.

We have seen that malice typically is not present in negligent wrongdoing, nor in purely instrumentally motivated wrongdoing. In contrast, malice clearly is present in the actions of many serial killers, including the Green River Killer, Gary Ridgway, who raped and strangled upwards of fifty sex workers because they were 'easy to pick up', and because he 'hated most of them'. Malice is a significant motivator in the actions of many murderers who participated in the Holocaust, in the Armenian genocide, in Stalin's purges, and in the blood-soaked reign of the Khmer Rouge. Many of these killers did not see their victims as people who, inconveniently, happened to be in their way. Rather, they saw their victims as corrupt and dangerous enemies who deserved death, or as inhuman vermin who needed to be extinguished. And this is precisely how Brenton Tarrant saw his innocent victims in Christchurch.

Hopefully you are beginning to see why malice is a plausible contender for being the psychological hallmark of evil action. For one thing, the presence or absence of malice divides wrongs into two categories. Malice is absent in many wrongs, but is present in a subset of wrongs, including in many infamous atrocities. Moreover, when malice is the motivation that lies behind a wrong action it exacerbates the wrong. Malice makes a wrong action morally worse than it otherwise would have been. The exacerbating effect of malice is reflected in the legal category of hate crimes, for which perpetrators receive comparatively harsher punishment and stronger moral condemnation. There is something particularly horrible about the fact that malicious wrongdoers are *seeking out* the opportunity to do harm, and that they want their victims to suffer or to be destroyed. In light of all of this, it is no surprise that some philosophers, including Lawrence Thomas and Manuel Vargas, believe that malice is a necessary part of evil action. John Kekes claims that 'evildoers cause more serious harm than is needed for achieving their [other] ends. They are not just unscrupulous in their choice of means, but motivated by malevolence to gratuitous excess. They treat their victims with ill-will, rage or hatred.' There are two important questions that we need to answer at this point. The first is whether the only difference between evils and ordinary wrongs is that evil actions were performed out of malice. In other words, is the presence of malice enough to tip any wrong action into the category of evil? If so, we would end up with the following definition.

> **The malicious wrongs account of evil action:** An action is evil if and only if it is morally wrong and is malicious.

The answer to this first question, pretty clearly, is no. There are plenty of morally wrong actions that are motivated by malice but that are still minor, inconsequential, or trivial. Imagine that the ill will you feel towards your rival moves you to tell a lie about her that embarrasses her in front of your friends. This kind of action is morally wrong, and is malicious, and it does inflict some harm on the victim. Nonetheless, it falls well short of possessing the requisite moral gravity to qualify as evil. Malicious actions are often petty, and the petty is merely petty. While malice is an exacerbator of wrong actions, the presence of malice does not automatically catapult every minor malicious wrong into the category of evil. But a second important question remains: Is the presence of malice a necessary condition for evil action? In other words, is it the case that every evil action was performed out of malice towards the victim? Advocates of this view concede that malice alone is not enough to provide the extremity that is required for evil action, and hence that we need to include an independent condition in our definition of evil that captures that extremity. However, they think that evil actions are the subset of extreme wrongs that are also performed maliciously. These philosophers believe that malice is what distinguishes evil actions from other non-evil but extreme wrongs. This gives us the following definition.

The malicious extreme wrongs account of evil action: An action is evil if and only if it is extremely morally wrong and is malicious.

This account may seem appealing, especially if we focus on the previously discussed examples of malicious serial killers and war criminals. Their actions are prime candidates for being considered evil, and these wrongdoers really did act out of hatred when they destroyed their victims. But we cannot test a philosophical definition merely by locating a few examples that accord with it. We must also look to see whether there are any cases that do not fit with the proposed definition. As philosophers put it, we need to look for counterexamples to that definition. In this instance we need to ask whether there might be some actions that do seem to be evil, but that are not extreme wrongs performed out of malice. Once we have framed the issue in this way it is not too difficult to zero in on the potential counterexamples. Sometimes extreme harm is inflicted on victims absent any malice. We need to ask whether any actions in which agents wrongfully but non-maliciously inflict extreme harm might count as evil. If we can locate some such examples, we will have undermined the claim that the psychological hallmark of evil action is malice.

One kind of case in which harm in inflicted without malice is when the harm in question is a foreseen but unintended side-effect of the agent's pursuit of another goal. Think of so-called collateral damage in a military drone strike. The collateral damage here refers to the nearby innocent people who are killed as a foreseen but unintended by-product of the killing of the intended target. The military officers who controlled this strike can rightly say that they bore no ill will towards these other victims. They did not hate them, they did not want them to die, they were not *trying* to kill them. After all, the military officers might say, they would have taken out their intended target without any further loss of life, had this been feasible. Yet to many observers the fact that the officers bore no malice towards these innocent victims does little to dull the strength of moral condemnation that they deserve. Their collateral damage killings were cold, callous, dehumanizing, and utterly abhorrent. Imagine a different case with a similar structure, one in which the board members of a pharmaceutical company know that their extremely lucrative new drug will have lethal side-effects in 5 per cent of customers, but choose to conceal this fact and mass-market the product anyway, resulting in thousands of deaths. The board members did not act out of ill will towards their victims, nor did they intend to kill them. They were just trying to make a profit. Nonetheless, their non-malicious action was wrong, and extreme, and worthy of our strongest condemnation. If foreseen but unintended mass killings like this are wrong enough to count as evil, then we ought to reject the malicious extreme wrongs account of evil action.

Those who want to defend the malicious extreme wrongs account could claim that non-malicious collateral damage killing is terrible, and is morally extreme, but is never evil. But an even stronger challenge to this account of evil action arises in relation to instrumentally motivated non-malicious killings. These are cases in which people are killed deliberately and intentionally as a means to securing some other desired goal. Some bank robbers kill civilians in the course of their robberies, shooting bank employees who refuse to comply with instructions, shooting witnesses who might be able to identify them in court, or shooting hostages as part of a negotiation. In contrast with the collateral damage killings, these murders are cases in which the perpetrators *were* trying to kill these inconvenient victims as a means of achieving their ultimate goal. They killed their victims deliberately and intentionally, yet this does not imply that they bore ill will towards their victims, or acted gratuitously, out of hate. The bank robbers did not target a persecuted group whom they reviled, nor were the robbers exacting revenge on people who had wronged or slighted them. They were simply doing what they needed to do in order to escape with the money.

If the malicious extreme wrongs account of evil action were correct, then no such actions could count as evil, on the grounds that they are not performed out of malice. This may strike you as the right outcome. Perhaps these kinds of instrumental killings are significantly less wrong than the malicious acts performed by serial killers. But how do you feel when we increase the scale of harm inflicted in these instrumentally motivated wrong actions? Imagine a case in which a large group of government employees accidentally discover a secret espionage programme that is being carried out by the government. For the sake of argument, suppose that this espionage programme is not actually morally beneficial, but that some members of the government mistakenly believe that it is very important. Imagine that the head of the secret police decides that these employees need to be assassinated, one and all, in order to prevent public embarrassment and to protect the programme, so summarily orders their deaths. He does not act out of malice towards his victims. He sees the killings as an unfortunate but necessary means to securing another end. Is this mass murder not evil?

By this stage you should have a grip on the ways in which we might argue back against the idea that malice is a necessary component of evil action. It is time to move on to consider the next contender for the psychological hallmark of evil action, namely, sadistic pleasure. This is pleasure taken in the suffering of others, or in the harming or wronging of others. Sadistic pleasure is closely related to malice. Those who bear malice towards us usually also take pleasure in our suffering, and usually enjoy wronging us. Despite the fact that they often go together, malice is distinct and separable from sadistic pleasure. Sometimes people bear ill will towards others but find that they do not enjoy it when they inflict harm on their hated victims. They may find the process of maliciously inflicting this harm unpleasant; perhaps it was frightening, or distressingly gory. In cases like these we might say that the perpetrators took nothing more than grim satisfaction in harming their victims, and this is distinct from the kind of gleeful pleasure that is present in many serial killers, and, indeed, in many playground bullies. Malice can be present in cases where sadistic pleasure is absent, and the opposite also seems possible. Sometimes a perpetrator might harm a victim not out of malice but merely as a means to securing another end, and then find, to her surprise, that she enjoys witnessing the suffering that she inflicts.

While several philosophers have proposed that malice is the psychological hallmark of evil action, some others have pointed to sadistic pleasure instead. It is easy to see why this might be appealing. Sadistic pleasure is an emotional response that is present in some but not all wrongdoing, and the fact that an agent takes sadistic pleasure in wrongfully harming the victim also seems to exacerbate the wrong. 'Not only did he torture the prisoner,' we might hear a horrified witness say, 'he *enjoyed* it!' A great many stereotypical evil villains from the realm of literature and film are conspicuous in their displays of sadistic pleasure. Film-makers typically tell their audience that a particular character is evil by depicting him rubbing his hands together or cackling with glee when contemplating his plans to inflict harm on others. This 'Mwha-ha-ha-ha-ha-ha!' cinematic trope is so familiar that it is an easy target for parody, as we see in the case of Dr Evil in the *Austen Powers* movies or Mr Burns in *The Simpsons*. Evildoers, we are being told, are not just wrongdoers; they are wrongdoers who *love it*. We should not make the mistake of supposing that this kind of psychology is merely fictional. Many serial killers—from John Wayne Gacy, to Ted Bundy, to the BTK killer Dennis Rader—take intense sexual pleasure in torturing then killing their victims. Some military torturers, initially ordered to do whatever it takes to extract information from their captives, develop a taste for what they are doing and come to seek it out. These are examples of appalling, terrifying, horrendous wrongdoing. They are prime candidates for being evil actions.

As is the case with malice, though, it is not plausible to claim that every wrong action that is accompanied by sadistic pleasure will thereby count as evil. Wrongdoers can take sadistic pleasure in the small amounts of suffering that are caused by minor, trivial wrongs. It is not evil to make a mean joke about your friend, even if you take pleasure in the fact that she squirms with embarrassment. The more attractive view is that sadistic pleasure is a necessary condition for evil action, and that the extremity of evil action must be included in the definition as a separate condition.

> **The sadistic extreme wrongs account of evil action:** An action is evil if and only if it is an extreme wrong in which the wrongdoer takes sadistic pleasure.

This view has its philosophical advocates, including Lawrence Thomas. The sadistic extreme wrongs account also has some support from outside academia. The psychologist Fred Alford interviewed prison inmates in order to discover their views about evil. He reports that many of the inmates believed that evil is 'pleasure in hurting and lack of remorse'. But once again, we cannot test a philosophical definition merely by looking for cases that fit with it. We must also look for counterexamples that might undermine its plausibility. In this case we should ask whether there are extreme wrongs that were not accompanied by sadistic pleasure, but that strike us as being evil nonetheless.

Perhaps the most powerful counterexamples to this view can be found amongst the actions performed by war criminals. Clearly many war criminals do take sadistic pleasure in the suffering of their victims. Yet there seem to be others in this group who perform terrible wrongs without pleasure, who experience nothing more than grim satisfaction in performing an unpleasant task that they mistakenly believe to be required of them. For example, philosopher Jonathan Bennett points to speeches made by the Nazi leader Heinrich Himmler in which Himmler acknowledges that the soldiers who had carried out mass shootings in aid of 'the extermination of the Jewish race' were engaged in a distressing and difficult task. Himmler said that these soldiers had undertaken a 'great burden' that required them to resist 'human weakness', and that they ought to take care to avoid 'suffering nervous breakdowns'. It seems plausible that at least some of the participants in the Nazi death squads did feel this way, and acted out of a terribly misguided sense of duty, without taking sadistic pleasure in mass murder. But many of us think that these non-sadistic mass killings deserve to be condemned as evil, even though the perpetrators found the whole process deeply unpleasant. In other words, not every evildoer is psychologically similar to Ian Brady or Dennis Rader, who got off on the pain that they inflicted. Some people do evil without joy. If this is true, then we ought to reject the sadistic extreme wrongs account of evil action.

A third possible candidate for the psychological hallmark of evil action is defiance of morality. Perhaps what distinguishes evils from non-evil wrongs is the fact that evildoers know that what they are doing is wrong, and do it anyway. Many wrongdoers mistakenly believe that what they are doing is morally right. These people break the moral rules, but they do not knowingly defy morality. In contrast, sometimes people give in to temptation, and deliberately do things that they know are morally wrong because, for instance, breaking the moral rules will allow them to make more money, or because breaking the moral rules will allow them to avoid a public scandal. These are people who knowingly defy morality, and do so for instrumental reasons. Another kind of defiance occurs in people who knowingly do the wrong thing *because it is wrong*, behaving like a delinquent teenager who wants to find out what the rules are precisely because he wants to break them. A prominent literary example of this kind of delinquent defiance can be found in John Milton's epic poem *Paradise Lost*, which tells the story of Satan's rebellion against God. Milton's Satan declares:

> To do aught good never will be our task,
> But ever to do ill our sole delight,
> As being the contrary to his high will
> Whom we resist.

Another famous example of delinquent defiance is found in Augustine's *Confessions*, when Augustine recounts his own childhood act of stealing pears from an orchard. Most theft is instrumentally motivated, but Augustine claims that his was motivated by precisely this kind of defiance:

> Yet I chose to steal, and not because want drove me to it.... For I stole things which I already had in plenty and of better quality. Nor had I any desire to enjoy the things I stole, but only the stealing of them and the sin.... I loved the evil in me—not the thing for which I did the evil, simply the evil: my soul was depraved,... seeking no profit from wickedness but only to be wicked.

Some real-life serial killers are also defiant of morality, writing taunting letters to the police, glorying in their violation of society's rules. David Berkowitz, the Son of Sam serial killer who shot and killed six victims in New York in the 1970s, wrote one such letter in which he described himself as 'Beelzebub', and which he signed off 'Yours in murder, Mr. Monster'.

Defiance of morality, just like malice and sadistic pleasure, can manifest itself in minor and trivial wrongs as well as in major wrongs. For this reason it would not be plausible to claim that every wrong action that is also defiant thereby counts as evil. The most attractive theory in this vicinity includes a separate extremity condition, as follows.

> **The defiant extreme wrongs account of evil action**: An action is evil if and only if it is an extreme wrong in which the wrongdoer knowingly defies morality.

As with the previous two accounts, this definition of evil has some
strengths. It picks out a subclass of wrongs, and it does so via a
property, defiance, that is an exacerbator of wrongs. It is a terrible
thing to lock up an innocent person against her will, but it is even
worse to do so while knowing that what you are doing is wrong.
The defiance of morality makes this action more deplorable than
it otherwise would have been. When we encounter wrongdoing we
often say, 'She should have known better.' But when it comes to
defiant wrongdoing, we say, 'She *did* know better, but she did it
anyway!' There seems to be something distinctively perverse and
blameworthy about defiant wrongdoing.

Both Marcus Singer and Roy Perrett have claimed that defiance is
a necessary part of evil action. There are some strong objections
to this view. The possible counterexamples to this definition
will be cases of extreme wrongdoing in which the wrongdoer was
not defying morality: that is, cases of extreme wrongdoing in
which the wrongdoer mistakenly believed that he or she was
doing the right thing. When we run through examples of
terrorists and war criminals, we see that a huge number of them
were violating morality but not defying morality, because they
mistakenly believed that they were acting in the cause of justice.
Indeed, many terrorists and war criminals see themselves as
moral heroes, fighting the good fight. Hitler and the other leading
Nazis showed no remorse. They mistakenly believed their
horrendous actions to be justified. Defiance of morality is an
exacerbator of wrong actions, but many of the most extreme and
most reprehensible wrongs were not performed in defiance of
morality. Not all of the worst real-life wrongdoers share the
distinctive psychology of Milton's Satan. Some people do evil
while mistakenly believing that they are doing good. This seems
to be a powerful reason to reject the defiant extreme wrongdoing
account of evil action.

The last of the main candidates for the psychological hallmark of
evil action is more complex than malice, sadistic pleasure, or

defiance. Roughly speaking, it is the silencing of considerations that should rule out performing harmful actions. When you deliberate about what to do you are weighing up reasons for and reasons against performing each of the various possible actions that are available to you. Some things typically count as good reasons for performing a given action: that you would enjoy doing it, that the action would be helpful to others, that you would earn money by doing it, that you would learn something by doing it, that you promised you would do it, and so on. Some other things typically count as reasons against performing a given action: that it would put your health at risk, that it would place an onerous financial burden on others, that you promised that you would not do it, that it would violate the rights of another person, and so on. Often an action has some reasons counting in favour of it while others count against it, and deliberation involves a kind of trade-off between competing reasons of differing strengths.

Imagine that the CEO of a corporation could choose to sell a particular product that she knows would massively increase the corporation's profits, but that she also knows would kill innocent people. The philosopher Eve Garrard contends that the fact that this action would cause deaths of innocent people is such a strong reason against performing it that the CEO should not even weigh up the possible profits that would be lost by failing to do it. Instead, Garrard believes, the fact that this action would lead to the deaths of innocent people should *silence* any considerations in favour of the action in the CEO's deliberative process. It should make the possible profits count for nothing in her mind. Virtuous people do not even engage in deliberation over whether to kill innocent people in order to take their money.

Garrard uses this view about silencing as a platform on which to build her account of evil action. She thinks that there is a qualitatively distinct psychology behind evil actions, a psychology that is not present at all in cases of ordinary wrongdoing. The evildoer, according to Garrard, gives absolutely no negative weight to the fact that the action would kill or seriously harm innocent people. The consideration that should rule out the action altogether does not even register in the eyes of an evildoer as being significant. Another philosopher, Adam Morton, proposes a similar theory according to which people who perform evil actions bypass a common motivational mechanism that in most people inhibits violence. On both of these accounts, the distinctive feature of evildoers is that, when deliberating over whether to perform evil actions, they are not at all moved by things that should immediately rule out the action in question. What sets evil apart from ordinary wrongdoing, on these accounts, is the fact that evil actions come from a precisely specified kind of insensitivity. Evil actions occur when the agent does not care at all about what should matter most.

> **The silencing account of evil action:** An action is evil if and only if the agent silences considerations that should completely rule out the performance of this action.

This kind of silencing is present in some but not all wrongdoing, and arguably it is an exacerbator of wrong actions, so it meets the basic criteria for being the psychological hallmark of evil action. Moreover, some of the *prima facie* examples of evil action fit this definition well. Think about the fictional serial killer Anton Chigurh, as played by Javier Bardem in the Coen brothers film *No Country for Old Men*. What strikes the viewer most clearly is this character's utter failure to care about the lives that he is snuffing out. What should distress him, what should hold him back, leaves him completely unperturbed. A similar lack of caring arguably is present in the actions of many war criminals, who carry out genocide without factoring in the moral rights of those whom they destroy. The Canadian serial killer Clifford Olsen, who murdered eleven children, provides a chilling example of this failure to be moved by what ought to be most morally significant. When asked what he would do if he were released from prison, he said, 'I'd take up where I left off.' When asked if he was not moved by the suffering of the victims' families, Olsen replied, 'If I gave a shit about the parents, I wouldn't have killed the kids.'

While these compelling examples of evil actions do seem to be cases in which the perpetrators silenced the considerations that matter most, in order to assess the silencing account properly we must also check for possible counterexamples. Are there cases of what seem to be evil actions in which the perpetrators did *not* silence the considerations that matter most? If we think about the broad range of perpetrators of genocidal war crimes, it is plausible that quite a few killed their victims while also feeling a non-zero amount of sympathy and concern for those victims. The *Einsatzgruppen*, the paramilitary killing squads who left a bloody trail through Eastern Europe during the Second World War, were not uniformly staffed by men who gave no weight at all to the lives of their Jewish victims. Historian Christopher Browning points out that many of the participants had moral qualms about what they were doing, but went ahead out of perceived loyalty to the group, or because they were ordered to do so. Some of the most awful and most extreme wrongdoing is carried out by people who give some weight to the things that genuinely matter, but who mistakenly think that these considerations are outweighed by other seemingly more important concerns. If the silencing account of evil action were correct, then only the *Einsatzgruppen* murders that were entirely wholehearted, that involved no deliberative outweighing on the part of the perpetrators, count as evil. This strikes many of us as being implausible.

Another problem for the silencing account concerns our ability to know when an agent silenced a consideration, as opposed to outweighing it in his deliberation. When we think about the mass murder committed by the *Einsatzgruppen*, how are we supposed to know which of these horrendous killings were performed by perpetrators who gave absolutely no weight to the importance of their victims' lives in their deliberations? How do we distinguish these actions from those that were performed by perpetrators who felt a little conflicted, and who were slightly worried about the suffering of their victims, but who pulled the trigger anyway? Should we say that probably some of the *Einsatzgruppen* killings were evil, but that we have no idea which ones? Critics of the silencing account believe that some of the most abhorrent wrong actions come from conflicted motives, and that these actions are evil even though they involve deliberative outweighing rather than deliberative silencing.

We have been considering the idea that evils stand out from ordinary wrongs in virtue of the distinctive psychology of the evildoer. Some philosophers maintain that this is true. As we have seen, though, they point to a range of quite different psychological features. Each of these purported hallmarks of evil action is an exacerbator of wrong actions, and this makes each account seem attractive to some degree. However, we have also seen that there are powerful challenges that can be raised against any of these accounts. If the concept of evil action is supposed to capture the class of the most extreme wrongs, then there is a significant cost to including specific motives in the definition of evil action. There are many distinct features of an action that can make it morally worse, including the severity of its effects. Thus we can always find examples of extremely wrong actions that lack one of the purported psychological hallmarks of evil. Malice makes a wrong action worse than it otherwise would be, but some extremely harmful and appallingly wrong actions are not malicious. Sadistic pleasure, defiance, and silencing also make a wrong action worse, but there are some extremely harmful and appalling wrong actions that are not sadistically pleasurable, nor defiant, nor entirely wholehearted. For this reason, some philosophers think that it is a mistake to try to define evil action via reference to the psychology of the evildoer. Instead, they think that evil actions can come from a very broad range of motives, and that not all evildoers are psychologically similar. This is the approach that we will explore in Chapter 4.

Chapter 4
The banality of evil

One of the most memorable phrases of 20th-century intellectual life, coined by Hannah Arendt in her 1961 book *Eichmann in Jerusalem*, is 'the banality of evil'. It has the pleasing ring of familiarity, and it is clearly supposed to be profound. When we hear it said, many of us sagely nod along. But what does it mean? In this chapter we will see how Arendt's famous phrase should be interpreted, and trace the influence of Arendt's analysis of the trial of the Nazi war criminal Adolf Eichmann. Arendt's claims about Eichmann have led some contemporary philosophers to reject the idea that the difference between evil and wrong must be qualitative rather than quantitative. They reject the view that every evildoer shares the same kind of distinctive, distorted motivational structure, and claim instead that evil actions can come from a broad range of familiar motives, and sometimes are performed by ordinary people like you and me.

Before we engage with Arendt's thoughts about banality, there is one final location in which we ought to search for a qualitative difference between evil actions and ordinary wrongs. This is the effects that actions have on their victims: in other words, with the kinds of harms that they inflict. Harms fall into distinct sub-categories: infliction of physical pain, maiming, enslavement, rape, public shaming, theft, removal of valued options, and so on. Could it be that evil actions harm their victims in a special way, a way in which victims are never harmed by ordinary wrongs? If this were true, evil action could be defined as wrong action that inflicts this special kind of harm. This is an attractively simple suggestion. In order to complete the theory all we need to do is identify the unique kind of harm that marks out evils from ordinary wrongs.

As soon as we start assessing candidates, though, the whole project falls apart. Is the distinctive harm caused by evil actions the death of an innocent human being? If so, then every wrong action that causes an innocent human death would count as evil, and every wrong action that does not cause an innocent human death would fail to count as evil. Both of these claims seem utterly implausible. Some wrong actions that cause human deaths are cases of culpable negligence or recklessness. No doubt these actions are tragic, grave, and serious, but how do they compare to a case in which a sadistic torturer deliberately inflicts terrible pain on a terrified group of captives for years and years without killing any of them? Does it really seem that the act of reckless manslaughter is evil but the repeated sadistic acts of torture are not? Perhaps the distinctive harm is something else: the destruction of the victim's will to live, or the failure to respect what the victims hold sacred. A torturer may well destroy his victims' will to live, and arguably what the torturer does is evil. Yet a suicide bomber does not destroy his victims' will to live. He simply murders them before they know what is happening, and arguably suicide bombing deserves to be condemned as evil as well. Alternatively, perhaps genocide is the distinctive harm that marks out evil. Genocide is a terrible wrong, and perpetrators of genocide do evil, but then so do serial killers, who clearly are not attempting genocide against any ethnic group. The problem is not only that harms vary in type, but that *serious and extreme* harms vary in type, and that some of the serious harms are simply quantitatively more extreme versions of mild harms. Any move to limit the definition of evil action to wrongs that produce a narrowly specified type of harm will be contentious, because there are bound to be other victims of other gravely serious extreme wrongs who would bristle at the suggestion that what was done to them was not evil. In light of these considerations, we should reject the idea that evils are the subclass of wrongs that produce a distinctive kind of harm. We need to move on to the next contender.

Some people believe that evil actions are distinguished from ordinary wrongs in virtue of their effects, but not in virtue of their producing a qualitatively different kind of effect. It is just that evil actions do *more* harm than ordinary wrongs. Several contemporary philosophers, including Claudia Card, Susan Neiman, and Paul Formosa, think that evil actions count as evil because of the magnitude or severity of their harmful effects, not because of any kind of distinctive warped psychology possessed by the perpetrators. These philosophers are deeply influenced by Hannah Arendt, or more accurately, by the view that Arendt held after 1960. Originally, in her 1951 book *The Origins of Totalitarianism*, Arendt claimed that the Holocaust revealed a 'radical evil' that could not be explained by the ordinary motives of 'self-interest, greed, covetousness, resentment, lust for power, and cowardice'. Arendt initially believed that evildoers must be psychologically different from the rest of us, that they must be 'demonic', or 'monsters'. This is the picture of evil that Arendt still held nine years later when she attended the trial of Adolf Eichmann. One of the key coordinators of the Holocaust, Eichmann oversaw the transport of millions of Jews via deportation trains to the death camps. He survived the war and fled to Argentina, where he was discovered and captured by Mossad and Shin Bet agents in 1960. In a daring covert operation, Eichmann was removed to Jerusalem, where he was put on trial for war crimes and crimes against humanity.

Along with many other observers of the trial, Arendt expected Eichmann to be a manifestation of 'radical evil', to be a 'perverted sadist', or an 'abnormal monster' motivated by extreme malice towards the Jewish people. What she saw in the courtroom was something quite unexpected. Eichmann was calm and mild mannered while answering questions. He showed no remorse, but also failed to take any responsibility for the mass slaughter. The decision to exterminate the Jews was made by his superiors, Eichmann maintained, and he was *just following orders*. Eichmann expressed this attitude clearly in his pardon plea: 'There is a need to draw a line between the leaders responsible and the people like me forced to serve as mere instruments in the hands of the leaders.... I was not a responsible leader, and as such do not feel myself guilty.' In her book *Eichmann in Jerusalem*, Arendt explicitly rejected the idea that Eichmann possessed a demonic or otherwise abnormal psychology: 'It would have been very comforting indeed to believe that Eichmann was a monster.... The trouble with Eichmann was precisely that so many were like him, and that the many were neither perverted nor sadistic, that they were, and still are, terribly and terrifyingly normal.' Arendt reported that Eichmann was not the kind of stereotypical villain who was motivated by malice towards his victims and who knowingly defied morality. What *was* striking about the mind of Eichmann was his thoughtlessness:

> Except for an extraordinary diligence in looking out for his personal advancement, he had no motives at all.... He *merely*, to put the matter colloquially, *never realized what he was doing*.... He was not stupid. It was sheer thoughtlessness—something by no means identical with stupidity—that predisposed him to become one of the greatest criminals of that period.

Arendt went along to the trial of Eichmann expecting to see a sadistic, malicious, and perverted monster, because this is what she thought an evildoer must be like. Once she came to believe that Eichmann was not like this at all, Arendt faced a choice. She could have stuck with her initial view that all evildoers act from motives of these kinds, and concluded that Eichmann did not do evil. But this was not Arendt's response. Instead, she maintained that Eichmann was an evildoer, and this forced her to reject her prior conception of evil.

Years later Arendt described this change in her view: 'It is indeed my opinion now that evil is never 'radical', that it is only extreme, and that it possesses neither depth nor any demonic dimension. It can overgrow and lay waste to the whole world precisely because it spreads like a fungus on the surface.' In *Eichmann in Jerusalem*, Arendt claimed that there is a 'strange interdependence of thoughtlessness and evil', and that Eichmann's testimony had revealed the 'banality of evil'. This is the phrase that has entered the public consciousness, that is repeated often in the context of analysis of the Holocaust and seemingly in every other journalistic or academic discussion of extreme wrongdoing. For example, after the 9/11 terrorist attacks Ward Churchill described the people who were killed in the Twin Towers as 'little Eichmanns', and it was clear what he meant. Churchill was implying that the victims may have appeared to be nothing more than bureaucrats with clean hands, but that they were actually culpable contributors to great wrongs, that they were so-called desk murderers who were complicit in genocide and terror.

Setting aside Churchill's provocative claim, we must ask whether Arendt was right about Eichmann and the banality of evil. When we say that something is banal, we are suggesting that it is ordinary, unremarkable, boring, or run of the mill. How could Arendt claim that evil—the most extreme, outrageous, horrific, appalling immorality—is banal? Some people, including the journalist Ron Rosenbaum, think that Arendt made an egregious error in coining what he calls 'the most overused, misused, abused pseudo-intellectual phrase in our language'. Rosenbaum's frustration is understandable. Saying that evil is banal seems to minimize its significance, to suggest that it is not worth close attention. This is something that neither Arendt nor her critics want to do. Even worse, there is clear evidence that Arendt was badly mistaken in her reading of Eichmann's character.

Philosophers and historians including David Cesarani and Bettina Stangneth have documented evidence of Eichmann's deep malice towards his Jewish victims. The public face that Eichmann presented in the trial was a carefully cultivated image of the obedient bureaucrat, whereas in 1945 Eichmann wrote that 'he would go to his grave satisfied that he had brought about the death of "5 million Jews"'. Later he said, 'had we killed all of them, the thirteen million, I would be happy and say: all right, we have destroyed an enemy'. These are not the words of someone who was thoughtlessly following orders. In this respect, at least, Arendt got things wrong. Eichmann himself was not an Eichmann, little or big, in the way that Arendt had imagined.

Given that Arendt was wrong about Eichmann's character and motives, what should we make of the idea of the banality of evil? Can we locate in Arendt's writing a series of claims about evildoing, and extract from them a definition of evil action? This task is surprisingly difficult because what Arendt says about evil is often unclear. In her defence, she was not trying to craft a precise philosophical definition of evil action. Arendt was a political theorist grappling with an overwhelming atrocity perpetrated against her own people, and she wrote about evil in a fairly impressionistic and metaphorical manner. At one point it looks as if Arendt might be proposing that the kind of thoughtlessness she claimed to have seen in Eichmann is the psychological hallmark of evil action. According to this view, all evildoers are thoughtlessly obedient in the way that Eichmann was. Yet this would be a highly counterintuitive definition of evil action, because it would imply that thoughtless, obedient bureaucrats deep within the engine of the Nazi machine would count as evildoers, but that the malicious and clear-sighted Nazi leaders who were driving the whole process would not. There are plenty of examples of serial killers, terrorists, and war criminals who think very clearly about the extreme harms that they are intentionally inflicting on innocent victims, and the absence of thoughtlessness does not render their actions anything less than evil. Ted Bundy had many failings, but thoughtless obedience was not one of them.

There is a more charitable way to construct a definition of evil out of Arendt's claims. Arendt was suggesting that not every evil action is malicious, or sadistic, or knowingly defiant, even though some evil deeds are all of these things. Her distinctive contribution to the debate on evil is the idea that some (but not all) evildoers act out of ordinary motives and without grasping the significance of their actions. Arendt believes that some (but not all) of the most appalling wrongs were not performed out of malice, nor with sadistic pleasure, nor in defiance of morality. This is what we should take 'banality' to mean in the context of discussions of evil. Saying that evil is banal does not imply that some evil actions are ordinary and unremarkable, but that some evil actions come from ordinary motives, and are performed by people who are not radical outliers in terms of human psychology. This view of evil has been accepted by a group of contemporary philosophers, all of whom agree that although some evildoers do fit the stereotypical model of the sadistic and malicious villain, many other evil actions are banal in the relevant sense. Having rejected the idea that there is a psychological hallmark of evil action, these philosophers believe that evils can be distinguished from ordinary wrongs in virtue of the amount of harm that they cause. Evil, Claudia Card declares, 'is not defined by motive'. It is 'the nature and the severity of the harms, rather than the perpetrators' psychological states, [that] distinguish evils from ordinary wrongs'. This gives us something like the following definition of evil action:

The extremely harmful wrongs account of evil action: An action is evil if and only if it is an extremely harmful wrong action.

The 9/11 terrorists qualify as evildoers according to this account, because they performed morally wrong actions that were extremely harmful, but so too do bureaucrats or corporate stooges whose wrong actions inflict extreme harms on innocent victims towards whom they bear no malice. Some evildoers have minds filled with hatred and vengefulness, other evildoers are thinking about meeting their targets at work and trying not to disappoint their bosses. As Arendt recognized, people are motivated to perform actions that are evil for many different kinds of reason. Evil actions are very wrong actions, and they are very wrong because of the extreme amount of harm that they inflict.

No doubt this approach will be frustrating to those who wanted the concept of evil to pick out something starkly different from ordinary wrongdoing. If evil action is simply very harmful wrongdoing, then there will be no sharp dividing line between ordinary wrongs and evil deeds. Instead, there will be a grey area containing actions that are somewhat evil, or borderline evil. Counterbalancing this cost, there is a real advantage to giving the kind of broad harm-based definition of evil action inspired by Arendt. It allows that there is great variety amongst evil actions, while still making sense of the fact that evil actions are the morally worst wrongs, and that they deserve our strongest moral condemnation. It seems obvious that more harm is morally worse than less harm, and much more harm deserves much stronger condemnation. While this seems like a sensible view, some challenges are waiting in the wings. We will now consider a series of objections that can be raised against the extremely harmful wrongs account of evil action, and see whether it is worth tweaking this definition a little.

The first objection focuses on culpability. I contend that it would not make sense to say to someone, 'What you did was evil, but it was not really your fault.' Judging that an action is evil includes judging that the agent is morally responsible for that action, that the agent is culpable, that the agent did not have a good excuse for having done it. Let us step back for a minute and think about the grounds on which people might fail to be culpable for doing what they did. Consider a case in which you are walking along the street and your rowdy friend pushes you from behind, so that you slam into a pedestrian walking in the opposite direction and knock her to the ground. In some sense it is true that *you* knocked this woman to the ground, but we would not hold you responsible for having done so. Rather, it is your rowdy friend who is to blame. He is the one who is culpable for the harm inflicted. In a range of other cases we similarly judge that someone who harms another is not culpable for having done so: when that person inflicts harm while sleepwalking, or inflicts harm while being coerced or blackmailed, or inflicts harm through an accident that could not reasonably have been avoided. In cases like these, the person who inflicts the harm ought to be excused, or partially excused, for doing so. We may even say that the person in question has not done anything wrong. A more contentious set of cases are those in which the person who caused harm acted out of ignorance. If a doctor had no idea that the medicine she was administering was highly dangerous, perhaps it would be inappropriate to hold her responsible for the harm that comes to her patients, unless, of course, she *should* have known that it was dangerous, in which case we might hold her responsible regardless.

It might not be obvious why these facts about excuses would constitute a challenge for advocates of the extremely harmful wrongs account of evil. This account already specifies that only morally wrong actions can count as evil, and we could simply add that evil actions must be wrong in the sense that the agent is culpable rather than excusable for what was done. Evil actions must, by definition, be the evildoer's fault. However, things do get a bit more complicated here. Sometimes an action is morally wrong, but the circumstances mitigate the agent's blameworthiness without fully absolving her of blame. Imagine, for instance, that a desperately poor single mother in Sicily decides to work as an informant for the Mafia as a way to escape poverty and provide for her children. The information that she provides ends up facilitating a significant number of violent extortions and killings. You might judge that this woman's actions are wrong, and extremely harmful, and that she is culpable for having chosen to participate. She should not have done it! But you might also believe that her prior state of desperate poverty is a mitigating circumstance. No doubt cases like this will produce a mixed range of reactions, but some people may think that this woman is nowhere near as blameworthy as she would have been had those mitigating circumstances not been present. Perhaps her actions, while extremely harmful, and while culpably wrong, were not evil, because she was not fully blameworthy for them. (Being fully blameworthy, in this context, does not mean being the only person who is to blame. Rather, it means being blameworthy to the full extent, rather than bearing significantly diminished responsibility due to mitigating circumstances.)

We also need to consider a similar set of cases in which we should hold a wrongdoer responsible for some of the harmful effects of her wrong action, but not for other harmful effects which were unforeseeable, or which were beyond her control. We could describe these as wrong actions that are unforeseeably calamitous. Imagine that you are in a bad mood, and in order to let off steam you decide to insult the bus driver as she is driving. This is a wrong action, and you are fully blameworthy for it. But suppose that the driver is distracted by your insult, and this causes the bus to crash, killing twenty passengers. It turns out that your wrong action was *extremely* harmful, and there was no excuse or even mitigation that might lower your responsibility for having done what you did. That is enough to make your action count as evil, according to the extremely harmful wrongs account. In reality, though, this action does not seem to be evil. In this situation we might say that you are responsible for the wrong action, but not responsible for its unforeseeable, extremely harmful effects. I think that the definition of evil action should be revised to exclude cases of significantly mitigated extreme wrongdoing, and to exclude cases of unforeseeably calamitous wrongdoing. This leaves us with the following:

> **The extremely harmful culpable wrongs account of evil action**: An action is evil if and only if it is an extremely

harmful wrong, where the wrongdoer is fully culpable for that harm in its extremity.

Next we need to consider some puzzles that arise in relation to the different ways that the harmful effects of an action can be distributed amongst victims. In the simplest case of a wrong action, there is a single victim who is harmed. In contrast, many wrong actions harm multiple victims. Think of the theft of jointly owned property, suicide bombings, the passing of an unjust law, and so on. The account of evil currently under consideration suggests that a wrong action will count as evil only if it inflicts an amount of harm that exceeds the threshold of extremity. When an action harms many victims, the question of whether it is evil will turn on how much harm it does in total. This seems unproblematic in the case of suicide bombings. The murder of each individual victim adds up to an immense amount of total harm. The problem arises in relation to actions that inflict only a small amount of harm on each individual victim, but inflict this small harm on a vast number of victims, and hence inflict an extreme amount of harm in aggregate.

Let us compare two cases of people who inflict pain on others. To help us make this comparison, suppose that a mild, slightly annoying pain that lasts for ten minutes counts as one unit of pain, and that a pain that is twice as intense counts as two units of pain. The first case for us to consider is a torturer who wrongfully inflicts, say, five million units of pain on a single person. This amount of pain is excruciating, utterly demoralizing, and traumatic for the sole victim. This action is extremely harmful, and uncontroversially is extremely wrong. The second case is someone who performs a single action that wrongfully inflicts one unit of pain on each of five million victims. One unit of pain is really quite mild and brief. But this second action also causes five million units of pain in total, so it turns out to be just as harmful as the first action. Nonetheless, many people would judge that this second action is much less wrong than the first, and would not

63

qualify as evil. Imagine if you could step in to prevent the first action or to prevent the second action, but could not prevent both? Wouldn't you choose to stop the torture of a single innocent person, and let millions of people endure a brief and mildly annoying pain instead?

The question of how to add up harms is philosophically difficult, and it is not merely a problem for those of us who are trying to give an account of evil. In response to the previous examples, you might be tempted to say that a great number of mild pains cannot add up to an amount of pain that outweighs an extreme pain felt by a single person, but this would be a surprising outcome. Why can't pains be added up? You are no doubt familiar with cases in which someone pinches you, inflicting some pain, and then increases the pressure, inflicting an additional amount of pain. If you concede that pains can be added up to produce more pain, you might try a different move. You could argue that the magnitude of harm (as opposed to pain) inflicted on the single victim in the first example can never be outweighed by the magnitude of total harm done to the many victims. Again, this seems odd. Perhaps the best response is to say that sometimes it is more wrong to inflict a harm that is over a certain threshold of extremity for a single victim than it is to inflict a greater aggregate of harm that is spread thinly over many victims. It is morally worse to hurt a single person a lot than it is to hurt a lot of people a little bit. This suggests the following revision to our definition of evil action:

> **The extremely individually harmful culpable wrongs account of evil action:** An action is evil if and only if it is a wrong that is extremely harmful for at least one individual victim, where the wrongdoer is fully culpable for that harm in its extremity.

I think that this is how we ought to respond to the puzzle of wrongs that inflict very many thinly spread minor harms, but this is a contentious view. No doubt many rational and well-informed people will disagree. They might say instead that actions of this kind *are* just as wrong, just as awful, just as worthy of prevention, as actions that inflict an extreme amount of harm on a single victim. This disagreement is connected to some real-life cases. How should we evaluate the wrongness of a politician passing a bill that makes the lives of millions of people slightly harder, when compared to a serial killer who ends the lives of only a few people, but does so in the most horrendous fashion?

Another puzzle that arises for this kind of harm-based definition of evil action concerns a set of actions that seem to be extremely morally wrong, even though they do no harm at all. These are cases in which people try to kill many innocent victims, but fail due to bad luck. Think about Richard Reid, the so-called shoe bomber, who in 2001 attempted to detonate a bomb hidden in his shoe while mid-flight in an airliner over the Atlantic ocean. Had Reid succeeded, he would have killed hundreds of innocent people. Fortunately, though, he did not succeed. While he held a lit match in his hand and tried to ignite the fuse of the bomb, other passengers intervened and restrained him. Reid's action did not inflict extreme harm, despite his intentions. What he did was gravely, seriously, and extremely wrong nonetheless. Let us call such actions harmless failed attempts. People are punished severely for harmless failed attempts, as they should be. When we focus on the question of moral responsibility, it is hard to locate a relevant difference between Reid's failed attempt at suicide bombing and a successful attempt. Reid was simply unlucky; the rainy weather on the day of the flight had dampened the fuse so that it would not burn. Philosophers who define evil action as extremely harmful culpable wrongs turn out to have committed themselves to the view that Reid did not do anything evil on that flight, because his wrong action did not cause extreme harm. My view is that we should include Reid's action, along with many other harmless failed attempts, in the category of evil. These actions are just as grave, just as worthy of condemnation, just as morally wrong, as many successful attempts.

In addition to harmless failed attempts, let us consider one more possible kind of harmless evil action. These are cases of what we might call extreme but harmless sadistic voyeurism. A voyeur is someone who likes to watch. A sadistic voyeur is someone who takes pleasure in watching the suffering of others. In reality, many sadistic voyeurs also enjoy causing others to suffer. Serial killers who torture their victims, such as Fred West and Dennis Rader, fall into this camp, and their extremely harmful actions are clear instances of evildoing. But what should we say about acts of sadistic voyeurism in which the voyeur does not cause or in any way contribute to the suffering that he is taking great pleasure in watching? Imagine someone who voluntarily and wholeheartedly takes intense pleasure in watching the extreme suffering of the victims who are trapped in the wreckage of car crashes, but only does so secretly, and only does so in cases where there is nothing that he could do to assist the victims. His action arguably is harmless. The victims do not know what he is doing, and hence are completely untroubled by it. Nonetheless, this kind of sadistic voyeurism, when directed at extreme suffering, is morally abhorrent. Some might say that this kind of behaviour is terrible, perverse, and repulsive, but not morally serious enough to count as evil. He is not hurting anyone, after all, nor *trying* to hurt anyone, nor putting anyone at risk. Others may be sufficiently appalled by this kind of extreme sadistic voyeurism to judge that this too is evil, even though it does no harm.

Suppose that we want our definition of evil action to include harmless failed attempts, and maybe even harmless acts of extreme sadistic voyeurism. This will require one final modification to the definition of evil action. What harmless failed attempts and harmless extreme sadistic voyeurism have in common is that both are actions that are connected in a morally bad way to actual or possible extreme harms. They are acts in which the agent either tries to inflict extreme harms or wholeheartedly appreciates them when they already have come about. We could capture this point by claiming that evil actions are *appropriately connected* to actual or possible extreme harms. (Of course, 'appropriately connected' does not mean connected in a morally good way to those harms, but connected in the way that is relevant to evil.) I have added so many conditions to the definition that the labels have become unwieldy, so I will present this simply as my final view:

> An action is evil if and only if it is a wrong that is extremely harmful for at least one individual victim, where the wrongdoer is fully culpable for that harm in its extremity, or it is an action that is appropriately connected to an actual or possible extreme harm of this kind, and the agent is fully culpable for that action.

This is intended to capture all and only the cases of the morally worst kind of wrongdoing. This may seem to be a fairly complex definition, but the general idea could be captured in the following slogan: evil actions are extreme culpable wrongs. If this is the nature of evil actions, then both religious believers and atheists can agree that evil exists. Belief in the reality of evil requires belief in the existence of extremely morally wrong actions of this kind, but does not require belief in devils or demonic possession. However, I am hoping that this definition of evil action is also attractive to people who *do* happen to believe in supernatural beings, and who may believe that some supernatural beings have performed evil actions. In this sense, I am offering a secular account of evil.

It goes without saying that my favoured definition of evil action is not universally accepted by other philosophers. Some of them believe that evil action should be defined in terms of the reactions induced in observers; evil actions are evil because of how they make us feel. Others think that Arendt was wrong, and that one or more psychological hallmarks of evil action must be built into our definition; evil actions are evil because they come from a distinctive set of warped motives. Some think that we ought to stick with a simpler version of the extreme harms account, leaving out the tweaks that I added relating to culpability, thinly spread harms, and harmless evil actions. I have tried to present and evaluate these alternative views fairly, but there is no doubt that my opponents would be inclined to argue back in defence of their own views. The debate over the nature of evil action is far from over.

Another possibility that philosophers ought to take seriously is that there is no single best account of evil action. As we have worked our way through the competing theories I have appealed to your intuitions as to whether certain actions are evil, or are morally worse than others, or are deserving of our strongest condemnation. This methodology often leads us to revise our views and to converge on a shared conception of the matter at hand, but it has its limits. Different people are bound to have divergent intuitions about at least some cases, and it is possible that these differences will persist after we have engaged in philosophical discussion of all of the rival theories and all of the relevant examples. If the level of disagreement is sufficient, we may end up accepting that there are several distinct but viable conceptions of evil action in play in everyday thought, and that no single one of these comes closer than its rivals to getting things right. If we accept this kind of conceptual pluralism in relation to evil action, then some seemingly substantive disagreements over whether a specific action ought to be condemned as evil will turn out to be merely linguistic disagreements; that is, they will be cases in which the disputants actually agree on all of the moral facts, and are simply using the word 'evil' to mean different things.

Even if we do end up being conceptual pluralists about evil action, the process of distinguishing and evaluating all of the competing definitions of evil action remains beneficial. We need to communicate clearly with one another when we evaluate extreme moral wrongs, and when we discuss how we ought to respond to these atrocious acts. When someone calls an action evil, it is very helpful to ask whether they mean to imply that it was influenced by a supernatural agent, or whether it was performed out of malice, or whether it was performed with sadistic pleasure, or whether it induces horror, or whether it is incomprehensible, and so on. By asking these questions, we are better able to figure out exactly what we are disagreeing about, and what counts as common ground.

Chapter 5
An evil person

We began this investigation into the nature of evil by engaging with a sceptical challenge. The sceptics believe in the reality of moral right and wrong, but they think that evil does not exist outside the realm of fiction, and hence they conclude that the concept of evil should have no place in contemporary moral thinking. In the preceding chapters I have set out what I hope to be a defensible secular account of evil action, according to which many real-world actions count as evil, including the atrocities committed by serial killers and war criminals. While this does address the question of whether evil is real, I have not yet engaged with another kind of objection raised by the sceptics: namely, that it is morally damaging and dangerous for people to think in terms of evil. In this chapter we will explore this particular sceptical challenge. I will try to show that it is connected to the question of what it would take for someone to be an evil person. As we shall see, there is a big difference between judging that someone has performed an evil action and judging that someone is an evil person. The latter judgement has additional implications, and is often made too quickly, without proper consideration of the evidence. I will claim that the genuine danger lies in this rush to dismiss wrongdoers as evil persons, rather than in the use of the concept of evil per se.

You may already be familiar with the idea that it is morally dangerous to use the category of evil. The knee-jerk condemnation of one's opponents as evil—thinking that 'Everyone who disagrees with me is Hitler'—is regularly mocked online, and rightly so. This kind of dysfunctional knee-jerk hostility shuts down debate, and blocks our ability to learn from disagreement. You may also be familiar with a more serious political criticism of those who use the language of evil to characterize social outsiders, including refugees and members of racial or religious minorities. According to this line of thinking, when we use the language of evil we demonize our opponents; we treat members of the out-group as if they were malicious beings who are scheming against us. We dehumanize them, holding them to be monsters or vermin. We write them off as things to be destroyed. Given that it is morally wrong to treat people in these ways, perhaps we have good reason not to use the language of evil. Some philosophers and historians, including Phillip Cole and Inga Clendinnen, also claim that people use the category of evil as a pseudo-explanation of wrongdoing. When we look at someone who participated in the Rwandan genocide and say, 'He did it because he was evil', we may falsely believe that we have identified the cause of his wrongdoing, and that no further explanation of the atrocity is needed. Thinking in terms of evil may prevent us from identifying the social and historical contributing factors that often lie behind extreme wrongdoing. It threatens to make us reactionary, exclusionary, vengeful, and cold-hearted.

This sceptical challenge focused on the moral danger of the concept of evil might strike you as being both more significant and more urgent than the claim that there is no such thing as evil in the real world. It suggests that the concept of evil is an infectious idea that leads to diseased and corrupted thinking, that we must purge the concept of evil from our minds or else do great harm to innocent victims. If it were true that using the concept of evil produced all of these terrible results, then we would have a powerful reason to drop it. But glancing back at the philosophical accounts of evil action that we have considered in Chapters 2–4, it is difficult to see why judging that an action is evil *would* have these effects. Let us start with the idea that using the concept of evil leads you to think of wrongdoers as inhuman monsters. I agree that we should not think of serial killers, war criminals, and torturers as dangerous beasts who are outside the sphere of humanity. Part of what it is to condemn an action as evil, I have claimed, is to judge that it is a culpable wrong, that the perpetrator is morally responsible for what he or she has done. Judging that a war criminal like Eichmann has done evil is actually incompatible with judging that he is merely a dangerous non-human creature who is not answerable to morality. Evildoers have shown a lack of humanity in the sense that their actions revealed a lack of kindness and respect for their fellow human beings, but denouncing their actions as evil is a way of holding them accountable as human beings, as rational agents, as wrongdoers.

Similarly, it is hard to see why judging that someone has done evil would lead us to write that person off as having nothing in common with the rest of us, as being beyond redemption, or as being automatically worthy of destruction. Philosophers who write about evil typically acknowledge that there are complex causes of evil actions, and that at least some perpetrators of horrific deeds undergo a kind of moral reform and come to feel deep remorse for their wrongdoing. A well-known example of a remorseful evildoer is the former Japanese soldier Takashi Nagase, who during the Second World War participated in the torture of prisoners of war. One of those tortured prisoners was the British soldier Eric Lomax, who survived to write an autobiographical book *The Railway Man*, subsequently turned into a film starring Colin Firth. In this book Lomax describes meeting with Nagase many decades after the war. Initially Lomax felt intense anger towards him, but eventually came to see that Nagase's remorse was genuine, and forgave him for what he had done. This should not lead us to judge that Nagase was not an evildoer after all. Rather, it suggests that some people who do evil are capable of reform and at least partial moral redemption. If this is a common view, why do Cole and Clendinnen believe that using the concept of evil will lead us to write people off, or to mistreat outsiders, or to shut down enquiry into the causes of extreme wrongdoing?

The key to solving this puzzle is noticing that there are two distinct but related concepts in play when we use the language of evil. First there is the concept of evil action, and second, the concept of evil person. Philosophers rely on this distinction when they assert that *not every evildoer is an evil person*. Roughly speaking, the thought is that evil actions are comparatively common, but evil persons are rare. An evil person is somehow especially bad, and is worthy of being written off. Just as an evil action is in the zone of the morally worst kind of action, an evil person is supposed to be in the zone of the morally worst kind of person. As yet, this is a fairly vague set of claims. We will spend the rest of this chapter exploring different ways that philosophers have tried to flesh them out and give a more precise account of what it is to be an evil person. Along the way we will re-engage with Cole's and Clendinnen's concerns about the moral costs of using the concept of evil.

The idea that not every evildoer is an evil person is one instance of a more general distinction between what we might call action evaluation and person evaluation. This distinction has received a lot of attention in the philosophical field of virtue theory, and it will be helpful if we take a brief detour through virtue theory before coming back to focus on evil. A useful entry point to virtue theory is recognizing that we often use one and the same word to categorize certain kinds of action and to categorize certain kinds of person. We might say that the civil rights activist Rosa Parks performed a courageous action when she sat at the front of the bus, and that Rosa Parks herself was a courageous person. Similarly, we might say that United States President Richard Nixon's actions when first he was questioned about Watergate were dishonest, and that Nixon was a dishonest person. If we consider only examples like these, it is tempting to conclude that everyone who performs a courageous action thereby counts as a courageous person, and that everyone who performs a dishonest action thereby counts as a dishonest person. Deeper reflection throws this into doubt. All of us tell lies at least some of the time, but it is also true that there are some people who are admirably honest and trustworthy, and others who are strikingly dishonest. An honest person can perform an isolated dishonest action without thereby becoming a dishonest person. There clearly must be some kind of connection between performing honest actions and being an honest person, but what could it be?

One possible answer to this question is that you count as an honest person if you have performed a great number of honest actions. Similarly, perhaps you count as a courageous person if you have done a lot of courageous things. We could call this an aggregative model of person evaluation: you count as an X person if and only if you have performed a sufficient number of X actions. Add them up, get over the threshold, and you belong in the category. There are some categories of person which appear to fit an aggregative model. You count as a champion Formula One driver if you have won a number of Formula One races, for example, and you count as a financial benefactor if you have donated a significant amount of money.

While this aggregative model of person evaluation is attractively simple, it does not seem to be the right model for the categories of being an honest person or a courageous person. One problem is that performing a large number of honest actions is not sufficient to make you an honest person. Even the most despicably deceitful con artist has told the truth on a huge number of occasions, when answering day-to-day questions, when letting people know what time it is, when planning misdeeds with co-conspirators, and so on. All con artists say a great number of truthful things, but we would not describe them as being honest people. Another problem is that someone might count as courageous even though she has not performed very many courageous actions. Imagine someone who is lucky enough to live in a very safe environment in which she is rarely ever in danger. She very rarely needs to resist fear in order to achieve her goals. Had she been placed in a dangerous environment, let us suppose, she absolutely would have resisted her fear and acted courageously. This is someone who has not performed a large number of courageous actions, but it seems plausible nonetheless that she is an admirably courageous person. She has courage, but has not been required to use it very often. When it comes to things like courage and honesty, the relationship between action evaluation and person evaluation does not fit the aggregative model. Being a courageous and honest person is not simply a matter of doing lots of honest and courageous things.

The main alternative to the aggregative model of person evaluation is a character-based model, according to which being an X person consists in having the character trait X. Arguably, being an honest person consists in having the character trait of honesty. Given that this is a morally good character trait, philosophers call it the *virtue* of honesty. There is much dispute amongst philosophers as to just how high we should set the bar for the possession of virtues such as honesty, generosity, and courage. For our purposes, suffice to say that an honest person is someone who not merely performs honest actions sometimes, but who is disposed to be honest when honesty is called for, and disposed to be honest for the right reason. An honest person is characteristically honest. She appropriately values truthfulness, and can be counted on to behave accordingly. In contrast, a dishonest person is disposed to fail to be honest on many occasions when it is important to be honest. Richard Nixon possessed a bad character trait—the vice of dishonesty—and he possessed this vice even though he did tell the truth on many occasions. This character-based model of person evaluation also allows us to make sense of the courageous person who has performed hardly any courageous deeds. Possessing the character trait of courage implies that you are disposed to perform courageous actions *when placed in the relevant circumstances*. Someone can have this virtuous disposition, yet very rarely manifest this disposition in courageous action, simply because she rarely finds herself in the circumstances where the relevant kind of action is called for.

With this basic knowledge of virtue theory in hand, it is time to return to thinking about the nature of evil persons. Several different approaches are available to us if we want to allow that not every evildoer is an evil person. The simplest way in which to conceive of an evil person is via an aggregative account which sets the threshold for being an evil person higher than having performed just one evil action.

> **The aggregative account of evil personhood:** You are an evil person if and only if you have performed more than a specified number of evil actions (greater than one).

Since some evildoers have only performed one evil action, this account allows that not every evildoer is an evil person. It also fits with the idea that calling someone an evil person is morally more extreme than calling someone an evildoer, because performing more evil actions makes you a morally worse person than someone who performed only one. Evil people deserve our strongest condemnation, not only because they have engaged in the most extreme kind of wrongdoing, but also because they are repeat offenders. Several philosophers have endorsed this kind of account, saying that evil persons are those who have done evil things repeatedly, or who do evil regularly. This may seem plausible. When you are asked to list people who you think are evil, you might point to Hitler, Stalin, or Pol Pot, and these are men who repeatedly and regularly performed horrendous misdeeds.

However, some problems arise if we conceive of an evil person in this way. If we employ an aggregative model of evil personhood, then we would have to say that anyone who has done enough evil to get over the threshold will forever remain an evil person, even if he later undergoes moral reform and tries his best to make up for what he has done. Some readers may well think that this is true for the Hitlers and Stalins of this world. But think back to Takashi Nagase, who repeatedly and culpably participated in evil acts of torture, but who many years later appeared to have undergone deep-rooted moral reform. It strikes me that the reformed Nagase does not belong in the category of the morally worst kind of person, even though he remains morally responsible for his terrible crimes. If you agree that the reformed Nagase is an evildoer but is not an evil person, then you ought to reject the aggregative account of evil personhood.

There are some additional reasons to think that the aggregative account gets things wrong. It is fairly common, albeit contentious, to explain why someone performed a horrendously wrong action by claiming that he is an evil person. Once Ted Bundy escaped from prison, for example, he quickly returned to murdering innocent victims, and we might try to explain this by saying, 'He did it because he was evil.' But this attempted explanation does not really make sense if being an evil person is simply a matter of having performed more than a certain number of evil actions. Then 'He did it because he was evil' would turn out to mean something like 'He did this terrible thing because he has done a lot of terrible things', which pretty clearly fails as an explanation. If we want to allow that 'He did it because he was evil' makes sense as an explanation, then we have a reason to reject the aggregative account.

Here is another problem for the view that an evil person, by definition, is someone who has performed a sufficient number of evil actions. According to this aggregative account, someone who performs only one evil action cannot count as an evil person. But what if we imagine someone with an intense and long-standing hatred of a persecuted minority group, who carefully plans and carries out a single malicious suicide bombing that kills hundreds of innocent victims from that group. This suicide bomber, having performed only one evil action, would not get over the aggregative account's threshold for qualifying as an evil person. If you think that a suicide bomber such as this could count as an evil person, then you have another reason to reject the aggregative model.

These difficulties can be avoided by switching to the view that an evil person is someone who has an evil character. Arguably the central component in an evil character would be the disposition to perform evil actions. So, according to this view, someone counts as an evil person because he is the kind of person who is disposed to do evil. But we immediately run into a problem here. Every evildoer must have been disposed to do evil, at least in some circumstances, because he actually did something evil, and you cannot do something without being to some degree disposed to do it. So if we try to define evil personhood via possession of a disposition to do evil, it looks like we will end up with an account which unhappily implies that every evildoer is an evil person. The solution to this problem is simple: we need to say that an evil person is someone who has a sufficiently strong disposition to perform evil actions. This is how we think of many other ordinary dispositions as well. By way of comparison, consider the disposition of fragility. Being fragile is a disposition possessed by many vases. Vases which are fragile are prone to break upon contact with a hard surface. Most thin glass or ceramic vases are fragile, but many other vases, including plastic ones, are not. However, imagine that I give you a plastic vase and tell you that it is not fragile, and you try to prove me wrong by throwing it violently onto the floor and stamping on it, or whacking it with a hammer, thereby smashing it to pieces. By doing this you have not shown that this vase was fragile after all. Being fragile is a matter of having a sufficiently strong disposition to break, or being particularly prone to break when hitting a hard surface. Some things which can be broken do not count as fragile, because they are not sufficiently prone to break in the relevant circumstances.

Drawing on this knowledge, we can build a dispositional account of what it is to be an evil person.

The basic dispositional account of evil personhood: You are an evil person if and only if you are strongly disposed to perform evil actions.

This account fits with the view that not every evildoer is an evil person, so long as we assume that many of the people who have performed one or two evil actions were not *strongly* disposed to do evil. Some people perform terribly wrong actions only when they are in very unusual circumstances, or only when they have been provoked into extreme anger. Their evil actions may strike acquaintances as being atypical, or not really like them. (Do not forget, though, that when we say that they are evildoers we are claiming that they are blameworthy for what they have done. The fact that they are not strongly disposed to do evil does not let them off the hook if they actually do perform evil actions.) In contrast, some people are strongly disposed to perform evil actions, in the sense that they will do evil in a broader range of circumstances, or will do evil more frequently when in the same circumstances, or will seek out the opportunity to do evil. Serial killers certainly fit this profile. So do many of the senior military officials and politicians who formulate the plans and issue the orders for genocide. These are people who did not stumble into doing evil. Evildoing is in their character. They do seem to be worthy of stronger moral condemnation than those who are only weakly disposed to perform evil actions.

This dispositional way of thinking about the nature of evil persons has immediately obvious advantages over the aggregative account that we considered earlier. First, the dispositional account allows that even someone who in the past performed a lot of evil actions might, having undergone moral reform, become a fairly decent person and not an evil person. The quality of your character at present does not always match up to what you did years ago, and the dispositional account respects this fact. Second, the dispositional account of evil personhood fits with the idea that

'He did it because he is evil' has the right structure to function as an explanation. What it would mean is something like 'He committed this atrocious action because he is strongly disposed to commit atrocious actions.' The philosopher Eve Garrard, a staunch defender of the concept of evil, worries that this is a circular pseudo-explanation, something akin to the famously ridiculed claim that opium puts people to sleep because it possesses 'dormative virtue'. Phillip Cole, who, unlike Garrard, is sceptical about the existence of evil, believes that nothing at all can be explained by this kind of appeal to evil personhood.

While it would be a mistake to think that 'He did it because he is evil' ever counts as a complete explanation of why someone performed an evil action, I contend that it can function as a partial explanation. Here it is useful, once again, to draw upon virtue theory. Think about explanations of lying. Suppose that someone said, 'She told a lie because she is a dishonest person.' This too might look like a circular pseudo-explanation. Sometimes the fact that someone told a lie is best explained not by pointing to the distinctive character of the liar, but to the features of the social environment in which the lie was told. Roughly speaking, we might say that pretty much everyone would have told a lie if they were in that same social situation. But on other occasions the fact that someone told a lie is partially explained by the fact that the person in question is a habitual liar, that she does not sufficiently value honesty, that she is markedly different from most other people in this respect. The fact that this person lied in a situation where most people would tell the truth is explained by the fact that she has the vice of dishonesty. Of course, this is not a *complete* explanation of why she told the lie. For one thing, a complete explanation would include an explanation of how she came to be a characteristically dishonest person in the first place. But, as the victims of con artists can attest, there *are* some characteristically dishonest people who lie much more frequently and egregiously than normal people do, and who are untroubled by their deceitfulness.

Similarly, if an evil person is someone who is strongly disposed to perform evil actions, then in some (but not all!) cases it will be true and useful to say, 'He did it because he is evil.' Of course, this will not be a complete explanation of the evil action, but no explanations in terms of character traits are complete explanations. If someone is strongly disposed to do evil, we can and should ask how he came to have that disposition. But this does not imply that his disposition cannot be an important part of the explanation of why he did what he did. Think about a serial killer such as David Berkowitz, the so-called Son of Sam, who wreaked havoc in New York in the mid-1970s. Consider Jeffrey Dahmer, who drugged, murdered, and then dismembered his victims, preserving some body parts and adding them one by one to his grisly collection. These are not people who unluckily found themselves in the wrong situation, who were pressured into extreme wrongdoing, or who acted against their own character. Not at all. Berkowitz and Dahmer repeatedly sought out and created the opportunities to kill innocent people, and took great pleasure in doing so. Their disposition to do evil was strong, by any reasonable measure. Not every evildoer is an evil person, but are you willing to say that these two are not evil?

The dispositional model of evil personhood has some strengths that the aggregative model lacks, so it is no surprise that several philosophers have defended a dispositional account. It does have some surprising implications, though. For example, the dispositional account implies that someone might count as an evil person because of his character, even though he has not yet performed any evil actions, simply because he has not yet found himself in the right environment. Advocates of the dispositional account tend to see this result as a positive rather than a negative. We are imagining someone who is strongly disposed to perform the worst kind of morally wrong actions, but has not yet had the chance to do so, like a misanthropic would-be spree killer who is lying in wait, biding his time until he gets his opportunity. This kind of person has a stronger disposition to do evil than is possessed by many of the people who actually do evil when they are placed in difficult circumstances. He is morally depraved, and deserves our strongest condemnation, so perhaps it is no mistake to say that he is an evil person even though he has not yet committed an evil action.

Some philosophers agree that a necessary ingredient in evil personhood is the strong disposition to perform evil deeds, but they think that there is more to being an evil person than merely having this kind of strong disposition. For example, Daniel Haybron and Peter Brian Barry have claimed that an evil person should be defined as the mirror image of the morally virtuous person. In this context 'the virtuous person' does not refer to a normal person who is decent and admirable on the whole but who is morally flawed in lots of little ways. Rather the virtuous person is someone who is morally excellent in every respect: a perfectly integrated moral ideal. If the evil person is the mirror image of this kind of moral ideal, the evil person would be someone who is bad in every respect, someone who not only is strongly disposed to perform extremely wrong actions, but who has no redeeming features whatsoever.

> **The mirror image account of evil personhood**: You are evil if and only if you are the mirror image of the morally virtuous person.

This is an attractive idea at first glance, but the metaphor breaks down as soon as we try to flesh out the details. Mirrors reflect visual images, and a person is not a visual image, so frequently there is no answer to the question of who counts as the mirror image of the virtuous person. Let us see how this kind of failure plays out. The virtuous person has well-integrated character traits that are directed at morally good ends, and that reliably lead her to do what is right. Her moral values are correct, coherent, and strongly held. Which kind of person would count as her mirror image? Is it a terribly misguided ideologue who has well-integrated character traits directed at morally bad ends, someone who is driven by a strongly held but misguided set of values? Or is the mirror image of the virtuous person an utterly impulsive and self-centred psychopath, who has a disintegrated character, who is pulled in all sorts of conflicting directions, who has no stable set of values at all? The metaphor of the mirror offers no guidance here. Consider another example: the virtuous person is someone who knows what she morally ought to do, and always acts in accordance with her own correct moral judgements. Is her mirror image someone who always knows what she morally ought to do, but who always gives in to temptation and acts against her own correct moral judgements? Or is it someone who systematically makes incorrect judgements as to what she morally ought to do, and always acts wrongly in accordance with her incorrect judgements? Again, the mirror metaphor provides no answer.

While these gaps are troubling, there is a further, deeper problem with the mirror image account. It implies that an evil person is someone who has absolutely no morally good qualities. This is an incredibly restrictive and unrealistic limitation. Think of someone like Hitler, who sought out and created opportunities to inflict unfathomable amounts of harm on victims who were in fact completely innocent, who did so over a sustained period, who was so deeply ideologically committed that we would have had no chance of reforming him. Was Hitler an evil person? According to the mirror image account, in order to answer this question we would first need to scour his record for any morally admirable actions, and search his character for any positive traits. If, for example, we discovered that Hitler had a warm affection for dogs, or that he properly respected and valued wilderness areas, or that he was regularly kind to his office staff, we would have to conclude that he was not an evil person after all. A mirror image definition of evil personhood almost guarantees that no actual person will count as evil. More importantly, it falsely suggests that Hitler's minor moral successes are crucially significant with regards to the question of whether he ought to be condemned as an evil person.

They are not. If you think that Hitler the dog-lover is an evil person, then you ought to reject the mirror image account.

Another extension of the dispositional account of evil personhood has been proposed by the philosopher Phillip Cole. It is worth saying that Cole himself thinks that evil does not exist. He maintains that there are no evil actions, and no evil people. Yet as part of his argument for this conclusion, Cole must tell us what characteristics someone would have to possess in order to count as evil. (The same kind of definitional burden falls upon atheists. In arguing for the view that God does not exist, atheists must tell us what they take the word 'God' to mean.) Cole suggests that an evil person would not merely be someone who is strongly disposed to perform the worst kind of morally wrong actions, but someone who was *born evil*. This is a familiar idea, perhaps most frequently invoked in relation to psychopaths, who are sometimes described as being innately evil. To be clear, what we are considering at this point is not the question of whether anyone is actually born evil. Instead, we are evaluating the definitional claim that part of what it is to be an evil person includes being born evil. Cole's view is that if anyone were an evil person, then, by definition, he or she would have been born evil. In order to prevent this from turning into a circular definition, we need to include an independent description of what it is that the evil person is born with. The best candidate is exactly the kind of disposition that we have been talking about earlier in this chapter.

> **The born evil account of evil personhood:**   You are an evil person if and only if you were born such that you inevitably would grow up to be strongly disposed to perform evil actions.

Is this a plausible account of what it is for someone to be an evil person? Let us begin by noting that this conception of evil personhood is almost always used to support what philosophers call an 'error theory' about evil persons. Consider the following analogy. Santa Claus, by definition, is a man who lives at the North Pole and flies around the world delivering presents to children on the night of Christmas Eve. Given that there is no such man in the real world, Santa does not exist. Countless children mistakenly believe that Santa Claus is a real person who exists, but all of these children are making an error. Similarly, advocates of the born evil account typically believe that an evil person, by definition, is someone who was born evil, but given that we know that the character of every human being is strongly influenced by his or her upbringing, we know that no one was born with a fixed evil character, and hence we should conclude that no actual person is evil. This view is often combined with moral arguments to the effect that it would be terribly prejudiced and unjust to suppose that some people are born evil, so it must be the case that no one is born evil. Sometimes it is also suggested that if someone *was* born evil, she would have had no chance of becoming a good person, and hence she should not be held responsible for her actions. But these additional arguments are typically treated as superfluous, because most of the advocates of this definition of evil action are sure that no one has a fixed character from birth.

It is fairly common to think that a person who is evil must have been born evil. This belief is often lurking in the background when people are worried that it might be morally dangerous to think in terms of evil. If we suppose that everyone who is guilty of serious wrongdoing is an evil person, and that an evil person is someone who is innately evil, someone who was compelled by his genes to become a torturer or a murderer, then we might end up embracing a kind of fatalism. What is the point in attempting to shape the moral character of children who have behavioural problems if these children were born evil? Better to write them off, perhaps. But giving up on troubled children is not morally defensible. Thus it can seem that the progressive struggle for the improvement of society is in tension with the use of the concept of evil.

These worries are understandable, but my view is that this line of thinking ought to be resisted. Even if the 'born evil' definition of an evil person were correct, it would not follow that thinking in terms of evil leads to this undesirable kind of fatalism. As we have seen, there is a significant difference between judging that someone has performed an evil action and judging that he or she is an evil person. All of the philosophers who have offered definitions of evil action agree with the claim that not every evildoer is an evil person. They tend to think that if evil people do exist, they are comparatively rare. In calling an action evil, you are morally condemning the action in the strongest possible terms and calling for the perpetrator to be held to account, but you are not implying that the person who performed the action was evil, much less that he was born with an innate and unchangeable character. Think about the Holocaust survivors, including Primo Levi, who claimed that evil was done to them in the camps. Do they assume that every camp guard was born such that this kind of behaviour was inevitable? Do these survivors assume that social conditions in Germany in the 1930s made no contribution to the subsequent mass slaughter, that the perpetrators were innately evil and would have done it regardless? On both counts, certainly not. Many people who use the word 'evil' apply it primarily to actions, and far less frequently to persons, and they do not assume that every evildoer could not have turned out differently. It is even possible to judge that many actions are evil but that *no one* is an evil person.

Truth be told, we do not know whether there are some people who are born with genes that always result in the development of this kind of character. Different pieces of evidence pull us in either direction. It is very difficult to change the behavioural trajectory of some children who from a young age exhibit so-called callous and unemotional traits, and despite our best efforts we often fail to do so. This supports the view that at least some people are strongly predisposed to become extreme wrongdoers. However, some genes which are correlated with extremely violent behaviour, including monoamine oxidase A genes, appear not to be inevitable causes of that behaviour. It looks as though the presence of these genes *combined with specific environmental conditions* results in the development of extreme antisocial behaviour.

In any case, the question of whether every evil person, by definition, was born evil does not turn on these empirical questions about the flexibility or fixity of human development. We do not have any good reason to accept this definition of evil personhood in the first place. If being born evil were part of the concept of evil personhood, then it would not make sense to accept that a particular individual is an evil person, but to continue to debate which life events caused him to become evil. Yet when we consider someone like Hitler, many of us do accept that he was an evil person while coherently continuing to argue over which events in his life turned him evil. Did Hitler become an evil person because he suffered from gas poisoning during the First World War? Or was it because he had post-traumatic stress disorder induced by his experiences in the trenches? Or did he become an evil person because of the humiliating beatings that he received as a child from his father? Each of these theories has its advocates. What matters here is not which, if any, of these explanations are correct. What matters is that it makes sense to argue over which environmental conditions contributed to Hitler becoming an evil person. When people are arguing over which life events turned Hitler evil, they are not assuming that every evil person, by definition, is innately evil. This strongly suggests that the born evil account does not contain the correct definition of an evil person.

When it comes to the question of the nature of an evil person, I have argued that we ought to reject both the mirror image account and the born evil account. Perhaps we should fall back on the basic dispositional account considered earlier. On this view, you are an evil person if and only if you are strongly disposed to perform evil actions, regardless of whether you have a few good traits mixed in with your extreme defects, and regardless of how you came to possess that disposition. This account suggests that not every evildoer is an evil person, but that people such as Hitler and John Wayne Gacy do count as evil people, on the grounds that they possessed particularly strong dispositions to perform evil actions. While this account is attractive in many ways, I think that it needs to be augmented with an extra condition. When we look at situations in which people step up their condemnation from 'What he did was evil' to the more extreme 'He is an evil person', they are not merely telling us that the person in question is highly dangerous and is likely to commit awful misdeeds when given the chance. They are also telling us that we should not try to reason with this person, or try to reform this person. They are telling us that this person is now beyond our reach, and ought to be treated as a write off. An evil person ought to be permanently constrained and punished, or perhaps even destroyed. When President George W. Bush called the 9/11 terrorists evil, he was implying that we should not expect that people like that could be talked out of what they intend to do. We should respond to an evil person not with empathy, not with diplomacy, not with attempts at re-education, but with force. In contrast, consider the claim that what Lynndie England did in Abu Ghraib was evil, but that she is not an evil person. Arguably, someone who makes this claim signals that there is hope for her, that she is not the kind of person who is forever going to perform actions of that kind when given the opportunity.

In light of this, my suggestion is that an evil person must have a strong *and highly fixed* disposition to perform evil actions: one that other members of the community do not have the power to change, one that we can expect to persist come what may.

> **The fixed dispositional account of evil personhood**:   You are an evil person if and only if you are strongly disposed to perform evil actions, and this disposition is now so firmly fixed that you ought to be treated as a write off.

The careful reader might suspect that I am backpedalling here. I previously rejected the view that an evil person should be defined as someone who was born evil, or who had an innately evil character, yet here I am claiming that an evil person has a highly fixed moral character. These two claims might look as if they are equivalent, but on closer inspection there turns out to be an important difference between them. I am claiming that an evil person is someone who has a strong disposition to do evil that is highly fixed now and into the future, not that an evil person had this kind of disposition at every previous point in his life, much less that an evil person was genetically determined to develop this disposition. Many of our mental and behavioural dispositions are not innate, but are the product of contingent experience and learning, and some of those learned dispositions, once acquired, are very firmly fixed into the future. Think of your ability to understand basic sentences written in English, or your ability to ride a bicycle. Neither of these dispositions is innate. Neither of these is an ability that you inevitably would have acquired, no matter what environment you grew up in. But once you have acquired them, both are very difficult to shift. Aristotle thought that virtues such as courage, justice, and generosity are not built into human nature, but are acquired via learning. Nonetheless, Aristotle believed, once you have been properly educated, virtue becomes second nature. Henceforth it is dyed into the fabric of your being. Clearly there is a difference between saying that a trait was innate and inevitable given your genes, and saying that a trait is now highly fixed or ineradicable. My claim is that the latter kind of disposition is necessary for a person to count as evil, but not the former.

If this definition of evil personhood is correct, we can make sense of the sceptics' fear that using the concept of evil will lead us to shut down communication with perpetrators, to favour destruction over diplomacy, to treat every extreme wrongdoer as a lost cause. If someone is an evil person, then we do not have a realistic hope of reforming him. The best that we can do is to constrain him and minimize his ability to wreak havoc. This is an incredibly high stakes judgement, the kind of judgement that often has irreversible consequences. For this reason we ought to be very careful not to rush to condemn wrongdoers as evil people. Instead we should ask ourselves whether we have good evidence that these particular wrongdoers are unfixable and beyond our reach. In most cases, while we might condemn the actions as evil, we should admit that we just do not know whether the perpetrator is an evil person, because we do not know whether he or she is beyond reform. To this extent, I am in agreement with the sceptics. Many of us rush headlong to condemn others as evil people, when in fact we should not write them off. But, as I have already argued, the judgement that someone has committed an evil action does not, in itself, have these implications. Condemning an action and calling for the perpetrator to be held accountable does not imply writing off that perpetrator. Many evildoers do not have firmly fixed characters disposing them to seek out the worst kind of wrongdoing. Many evildoers come to feel remorse, many subsequently undergo moral reform. The sceptics have pointed out a good reason to be very cautious in judging that someone is an evil person, but they have not given us reason to believe that we ought to stop using the concept of evil altogether.

Chapter 6
Are you evil? Is anyone evil?

We have been trying to figure out what counts as an evil action, and which is the best definition of an evil person. I want to begin this brief final chapter by turning the spotlight on you. Are you a potential evildoer? Even worse, could you be an evil person? It is very tempting to respond to these questions with a flat denial. When we evaluate ourselves, most of us claim to have fairly strong moral values, albeit vitiated by a few weaknesses. Extreme wrongs are performed only by people who lack moral values, people who have no conscience, not by decent folk like us. Granted, many of us recognize that if we were placed under extreme duress, our resolve might crumble and we might inflict extreme harm on others. If we were threatened or blackmailed, if we were starving and desperate for food, if we were falsely accused and unjustly incarcerated, or if the lives of our loved ones were at risk, we might use violence in order to get what we needed. But these kinds of desperate circumstances are typically taken to mitigate responsibility for wrongdoing. You are not fully culpable for what you do when you are in these kinds of situation, and we have already decided that evil actions, by definition, are actions for which the agent is fully culpable. So the fact that you are disposed to inflict harm on others when you are in exculpatory circumstances does not imply that you are an evildoer in waiting, or that you are an evil person. However, there is a more worrying challenge lurking in this vicinity. In the 1960s the psychologist

Stanley Milgram carried out a ground-breaking set of experiments that tested our tendency to obey authority figures. What he found was surprising and appalling. Milgram's discovery suggests that most of us are disposed to inflict terrible harm on others even when we are not in desperate circumstances.

If you had signed up to participate in Milgram's obedience experiment, here is what would have happened. Upon your arrival at the designated room on a university campus, a scientist wearing a lab coat would have told you (falsely) that you were taking part in an experiment that tested whether punishment has a positive impact on learning. You had randomly been assigned the role of 'teacher', the scientist would say, whereas another person who had signed up was going to play the role of 'learner'. You would have seen the learner being strapped into a chair, and watched as electrodes were attached to his body. Then you would have been led into another room and seated in front of a machine featuring a long row of electrical switches, starting at 45 volts and moving in incremental steps all the way up to 450 volts. You would have been given a sample low-voltage shock yourself, to show you how much it hurt, and then the experimenter would have explained the learning procedure. Your job as the teacher would be to read out pairs of words to the learner and then test his ability to remember them. Every time the learner in the other room made a mistake, you would push down a switch and give him an electric shock as punishment. After each wrong answer you would be required to move one step up the scale to a higher voltage. If you expressed doubts about what you were doing during the course of the experiment, or if you said that you wanted to check to see if the learner was OK, the scientist would have told you that no lasting damage was being done to the learner, and that the experiment required that you continue. If you repeatedly expressed the decision to stop, the scientist would have allowed you to stop at any stage.

This sounds more than a little bit nasty. Even mild electric shocks hurt. As you move up the scale, they become not only overwhelmingly painful, but life-threatening. You are not the kind of person who would give excruciating and potentially deadly electric shocks to an innocent stranger, are you? When contemplating this scenario in advance, most of us say that we would not comply with the experimenter's instructions, especially not beyond the point at which the learner in the next room was crying out in pain and begging to be released. Surely we are compassionate. We care about the well-being of the learner, and we have no desire for him to suffer. Surely we are courageous enough to stand up to the scientist. After all, the scientist is not threatening us in any way, or imposing any costs on us. The scientist is merely instructing us to continue.

The terrible discovery made by Milgram is that most people continue to administer the electric shocks well beyond the point at which the learner is crying out and begging to be released. (In the Milgram experiment, there is no actual electrocution going on. The learner is an actor, and the screams that the teacher hears from the next room are faked, but they are convincing enough to fool the vast majority of the participants.) In Milgram's version 65 per cent of participants administered the shocks beyond the point at which the distressed learner had fallen silent, and continued right up to the highest point on the scale, 450 volts. They did not follow the scientist's instructions with gleeful sadism. Nor did they obey in a cold dispassionate manner. Rather, most of them obeyed while showing signs of distress, while asking after the well-being of the learner who they could hear screaming in the next room, and while expressing doubts as to whether the whole process was justified. They obeyed, it seems, while knowing that they should do otherwise. Most people in this setting are so obedient that they are willing to betray their own values and electrocute the learner to the point at which they believe that they may have killed him, or at least tortured him beyond the point of consciousness.

You might be reading this and thinking to yourself, 'Yes, but I wouldn't do that. I have a strong conscience. I would refuse early on.' The scary fact of the matter is that the majority of people tell themselves exactly the same thing, but go ahead and electrocute the learner as instructed. This experiment has been replicated many times with widely varied groups of people, and the rate of obedience fluctuates only a little. Chances are that you too are disposed to electrocute an innocent stranger to death when an authority figure is telling you to punish him for having made mistakes on a trivial memory task. This would be an extremely immoral thing to do, and what excuse could you offer in your defence? That the man in the white coat told you to do it? 'I was just following orders' was ridiculed at the Nuremberg trials of Nazi war criminals, so it is not clear why we should accept it here. When the order issued is clearly immoral, you should not follow it. There is a strong case to be made for the conclusion that electrocuting an innocent person to death in these circumstances is wrong enough to be evil. The upshot of this is that both you and I are quite likely disposed to do evil when placed in a Milgram scenario.

No doubt this is a sobering thought. Some might go scrambling back to definitions of evil which imply that malice or sadistic pleasure are required for an action to count as evil. Since the subjects in the Milgram experiment did not act out of malice towards the learner and did not take sadistic pleasure in the learner's suffering, their actions could not be evil, at least on these more restrictive definitions. Yet, as we have seen, the cost of these restrictive definitions is that they imply that non-malicious 'desk murderers' never do evil. If you think that non-malicious but culpable contributions to genocide should be condemned as evil, you need to stick with a broader, more inclusive definition. The philosopher John Doris has claimed that the Milgram experiment provides clear evidence that none (or almost none) of us is morally virtuous, in Aristotle's sense of having a robust good character that disposes us to act rightly across a broad range of environments. Doris's pessimistic reaction is opposed by several others, who for a range of reasons are keen to downplay the significance of our failure in Milgram scenarios. Some claim that, since most of us would obey these kinds of orders, the gentle pressure exerted by the scientist *does* count as exculpatory, and we are not really blameworthy for what we do in these situations. Some suggest that because most of the subjects in the Milgram experiment felt terrible about what they were doing, they may have been virtuous people after all. Some claim that Milgram scenarios are vanishingly rare in the real world, and hence that ordinary people are not prone to extreme wrongdoing in the situations that matter. None of these responses is very comforting.

There is at least some good news in relation to our tendency to obey instructions that we ourselves know to be immoral. Milgram discovered that most people very quickly opt out of administering the shocks as soon as someone else in the room speaks up and contradicts the scientist or suggests that they ought to go and check on the learner. We are afraid of embarrassment, of being the one to speak out when others seem to know what they are doing. What is hard to disobey is not an authority figure per se, but an *uncontradicted* authority figure. But this piece of good news is counterbalanced by the fact that people are strongly inclined to go along with the behaviour of a group, when the members of that group are all in agreement, even if the group does not contain an authority figure. While Milgram scenarios might well be rare in the real world, more frequent are cases in which a group carries out extreme wrongdoing, including persecution of minorities. Many of us are vulnerable to being swept along with this behaviour against our own better judgement because we do not want to be the one who steps out of line. We are alarmingly weak-willed in the face of authorities and unified groups. If we want to avoid doing evil, we need to be vigilant in monitoring our own behaviour when in these kinds of situations. We need to be more willing to speak up and to step out of line.

We are also at risk of doing evil when our moral judgements are inaccurate, when we mistakenly believe that our targets deserve to be harmed or even destroyed. This can happen when we fall into the grip of an ideology which demonizes its innocent opponents, which leads us to judge that apostates deserve to be stoned to death, or that Federal Government workers are legitimate targets of bombings, or that sex workers ought to be killed as punishment. Many of us can be whipped into a vindictive and self-righteous rage, and then lash out impulsively. But it is also too easy for us to make intellectual errors, and perform terribly immoral actions in a cool, calm, and collected fashion, grim in our certitude. There is no easy answer to the question of how best to avoid falling into the grip of a mistaken moral worldview. Reflection, dialogue, and imaginative engagement with others are all useful tools for revising our moral judgements. We cannot opt out of making moral judgements altogether, nor should we. We must strive to make our moral judgements carefully, from an informed perspective, on the basis of the relevant evidence.

I have claimed that ordinary people have a greater capacity for evildoing than we like to admit. If this is true, does it imply that most of us are evil people? According to the definition that I offered in Chapter 5, an evil person is someone who has a strong and highly fixed disposition to perform evil actions, someone who is beyond hope of reform. There are two reasons why we should doubt the claim that most of us are evil. The first is that ordinary people do not have a particularly strong disposition to perform evil actions, at least in most situations. Ordinary people do not seek them out, and do not leap into evildoing at the slightest provocation, although many of us are liable to do terrible wrongs when pressured. The second reason that we should not conclude that most ordinary people are evil is that we do not have good reason to think that our dispositions towards wrongdoing cannot be altered. Ordinary people who do evil should not be written off because they can see that they have done the wrong thing, they feel remorse, they learn from their mistakes, and they resolve not to fall into that trap again. By becoming aware of our susceptibility to authority figures and unified mobs, we can guard against our own worst tendencies. We can improve.

Some philosophers believe so fervently in the power of humans to learn and improve that they reject the idea that anyone is an evil person. Phillip Cole, for example, claims that every wrongdoer is redeemable, and hence that no one should be treated as a lost cause. This sentiment is admirable in some respects. It certainly is true that when we encounter someone who has performed an appalling action we ought to hope that his character is not so firmly fixed that he will continue doing these things come what may. When a soldier sadistically tortures a captive enemy combatant we ought to hope that this soldier is not the kind of person who will always brutalize those whom he sees as the enemy. We ought to encourage this soldier to feel remorse, to apologize, to undergo moral reform, to become the kind of person who would not administer this kind of torture. We ought to look for evidence that he has reformed, and we ought to factor any such evidence in to our assessment of the soldier's character and his prospects for the future. When a teenager commits a horrific murder we ought not to jump to the conclusion that murder is in his blood, that he is always bound to wreak havoc on those around him, that he should be locked up forever. We ought to hope that he can escape the social world that contributed to his terrible wrongdoing, and that he can cultivate the better side of his character to the extent that he is no longer a risk to others.

It is reasonable to have these hopes, and we should be ready to respond to evidence that these hopes are coming true. Nonetheless, I think that it is dangerous to believe that no one is evil, and that no one should be written off. Some evildoers give us clear evidence that they are unrepentant, that they remain strongly disposed to perform the morally worst kinds of actions, and that they are highly resistant to our best attempts to lead them into a process of moral reform. This is sometimes true in the case of ideologically committed war criminals, who, despite being captured and tried, maintain their innocence and their commitment to the cause. Evidence of recalcitrance is even clearer in the case of some serial killers, who continue to commit their crimes for years, even decades. In 1977, after carrying out a stream of carefully planned abductions, rapes, and murders, Ted Bundy was imprisoned for kidnapping. He escaped from a Colorado courthouse, and after six days on the run he was recaptured. But once in jail he hatched another escape plan. He starved himself to lose weight, sawed a hole in the ceiling of his cell, and managed to squeeze through. Free again, Bundy fled to Chicago then on to Florida, where he quickly returned to abducting and murdering women. He only admitted his responsibility for his crimes after he had been convicted. Did he feel any remorse for what he had done? Seemingly not. In 1981 Bundy said, 'I guess I am in the enviable position of not having to deal with guilt.' It is beyond doubt that this is a man who was strongly disposed to perform the most abhorrent wrongs. Was Ted Bundy fixable? Was he redeemable? Could we have helped him become a good person? Engaging in wishful thinking is not always pathological, but here I think it is. Bundy revealed through his actions, again and again, who he was. He deserved to be written off. He was not just an evildoer, but an evil person.

Some evildoers are remorseful, but repeatedly demonstrate by their behaviour that they are recalcitrant nonetheless. If we have learned anything from the terrifying systemic sexual abuse committed by priests in the Catholic Church, it is that we need to exercise great care in deciding whether to trust those who confess, express remorse, and ask for forgiveness. Some evildoers seem to be set on their course, regardless of their own self-conception as sinners who have turned a corner and are now on the road to redemption. The best we can do in cases like these is to punish the perpetrators and to minimize the threat that they pose to others, rather than to treat them as lost lambs who just need acceptance and love.

Genuine moral reform is possible for some evildoers, but it can be very difficult for observers to figure out when we have encountered the real thing. In 1976 Jack Unterweger was imprisoned in Austria for strangling 18-year-old Margaret Schäfer to death. While in jail he appeared to undergo a moral rebirth, writing an autobiography and other works that detailed his rehabilitation. He became a *cause célèbre*, as a collection of novelists, artists, and political activists lobbied the government for his release. After being set free in 1990 Unterweger continued to build his media profile, hosting television programmes and working for the Austrian public broadcaster. He even visited Los Angeles as a journalist, commissioned to write about crime and prostitution in the USA. Tragically, Unterweger's highly publicized reform was a ruse. After his release from prison he murdered a further eleven women, including three in Los Angeles. In 1992 he was captured, and in 1994 he was convicted and sentenced to life without parole. That night, he hanged himself in his cell, tying the noose with the same knot that he had used when strangling his victims. Unterweger, like Bundy, ultimately gave us good reason to believe that he was beyond reform. His most audacious act was convincing so many that he had made good, when in fact he remained, to his death, evil.

References

Chapter 1: The philosophical puzzle of evil

The Ludwig Wittgenstein quote comes from his 1953 book *Philosophical Investigations*, trans. G. E. Anscombe, Oxford: Basil Blackwell, section 593.

Felicia Sanders's comment about Dylann Roof can be found in Kevin Sullivan's article '"Evil, evil, evil as can be": emotional testimony as Dylann Roof trial begins', *The Washington Post*, 7 December 2016. <https://www.washingtonpost.com/news/postnation/wp/2016/12/07/as-dylann-roof-trial-begins-prosecutordescribes-each-victims-life-and-how-they-died/>.

Janne Kristiansen's assessment of Breivik can be found in Karl Ritter and Ian MacDougall's article 'Police to question mass killer Breivik again', *The Independent*, 28 July 2011. <https://www.independent.co.uk/news/world/europe/police-to-question-mass-killerbreivik-again-2327510.html>.

Barack Obama's claim can be found in Julian Borger and Patrick Wintour's article 'Obama vows to destroy Isis's "brand of evil" as Iraq requests help from Britain', *The Guardian*, 25 September 2014. <https://www.theguardian.com/world/2014/sep/24/obama-isisbrand-of-evil-uk-air-strikes-iraq>.

Donald Trump's comment comes from Peter Beaumont's article 'Donald Trump says "evil losers" were behind Manchester attack', *The Guardian*, 23 May 2017. <https://www.theguardian.com/usnews/2017/may/23/donald-trump-evil-losers-manchester-attack>.

Tony Blair's comment comes from Michael White, Alan Travis, and Duncan Campbell's article 'Blair: uproot this ideology of evil', *The Guardian*, 14 July 2005. <https://www.theguardian.com/politics/2005/jul/14/religion.july7>.

David Cameron's comment comes from an article that he published in *The Telegraph* on 22 November 2015, 'David Cameron: we will defeat terrorism, and the poisonous ideology that fuels it'. <https://www.telegraph.co.uk/news/uknews/defence/12010788/David-Cameron-We-will-defeat-terrorism-and-thepoisonous-ideology-that-fuels-it.html>.

Polly Nelson's claim comes from her book *Defending the Devil: My Story as Ted Bundy's Last Lawyer*, New York: William Morrow, 1994.

The media comment about Myra Hindley comes from the article 'Hindley: I wish I'd been hanged', *BBC News*, 29 February 2000. <http://news.bbc.co.uk/2/hi/uk_news/661139.stm>.

Hannah Arendt's comment about the banality of evil comes from *Eichmann in Jerusalem*, New York: Penguin, 2006.

Christopher Hitchens's claim about evil comes from his article 'Evil', *Slate*, 31 December 2002. <https://slate.com/news-and-politics/2002/12/the-necessity-of-evil.html>.

Chapter 2: The horror and incomprehensibility of evil action

Elizabeth Warren posted her comment on Twitter on 21 April 2019.

Chapter 3: The psychological hallmark of evil action

Arendt's claims about radical evil come from her book *The Origins of Totalitarianism*, London: Allen and Unwin, 1967, p. 459.

The quote from John Kekes comes from *The Roots of Evil*, Ithaca, NY: Cornell University Press, 2005, p. 2.

Fred Alford describes his study of prison inmates in his book *What Evil Means to Us*, Ithaca, NY: Cornell University Press, 1997.

Roy Perrett discusses Alford's study in his paper 'Evil and human nature', *The Monist*, 85.2 (2002), p. 306.

The quoted sections of Himmler's speech can be found in Jonathan Bennett, 'The conscience of Huckleberry Finn', *Philosophy*, 49.188 (1974), p. 128.

The quoted section from John Milton's poem *Paradise Lost* comes from Bk I, 159–62.

The quotation from Augustine's *Confessions* comes from Book 2, IV.
Clifford Olsen's comments are recounted in Michael Stone's book *The Anatomy of Evil*, New York: Prometheus Books, 2009, p. 350.

Chapter 4: The banality of evil

The quote from Arendt's book *The Origins of Totalitarianism*, originally published in 1951, comes from the republished 1967 version (London: Allen and Unwin), p. 459.

The quotes from Arendt's book *Eichmann in Jerusalem*, originally published in 1961, come from the republished 2006 version (New York: Penguin), pp. 276, 276, 287–8, 288, and 252, respectively.

The later quotation in which Arendt compares evil to a fungus comes from *The Jew as Pariah*, New York: Grove, 1978, p. 251.

The quote from Eichmann's pardon plea can be found in Isabel Kershner's article 'Pardon plea by Adolf Eichmann, Nazi war criminal, is made public', *The New York Times*, 27 January 2016.

Ward Churchill's claim about 'little Eichmanns' can be found in *On the Justice of Roosting Chickens: Reflections on the Consequences of U. S. Imperial Arrogance and Criminality*, New York: AK Press, 2003.

Ron Rosenbaum's comment comes from his article 'The evil of banality', *Slate*, 30 October 2009. <www.slate.com/articles/life/the_spectator/2009/10/the_evil_of_banality.html>.

Eichmann's claims are quoted in David Cesarani's book *Becoming Eichmann: Rethinking the Life, Crimes, and Trial of a 'Desk Murderer'*, London: De Capo Press, 2004, pp. 300 and 360, respectively.

The quotations from Claudia Card can be found in her book *The Atrocity Paradigm*, New York: Oxford University Press, 2002, pp. 9 and 3.

Chapter 6: Are you evil? Is anyone evil?

The Ted Bundy quotation comes from a book by Stephen Michaud and Hugh Aynesworth, *The Only Living Witness: The True Story of Serial Sex Killer Ted Bundy*, Irving, TX: Authorlink Press, 1999, p. 281.

Further reading

The dispute between historians regarding the motives of ordinary Germans is played out in:

Daniel Goldhagen's (1997) book *Hitler's Willing Executioners: Ordinary Germans and the Holocaust*, New York: Random House.

Christopher Browning's (1998) book *Ordinary Men: Reserve Police Battalion 101 and the Final Solution in Poland*, New York: HarperCollins.

Philosophers discuss the view that evil is qualitatively distinct from ordinary wrongdoing in the following articles:

Todd Calder (2013), 'Is evil very wrong?', *Philosophical Studies*, 163: 177–96.

Stephen de Wijze (2002), 'Defining evil: Insights from the problem of "dirty hands"', *The Monist*, 85.2: 210–38.

Eve Garrard (1998), 'The nature of evil', *Philosophical Explorations*, 1: 43–60.

Daniel Haybron (2002), 'Moral monsters and moral saints', *The Monist*, 85.2: 260–84.

Luke Russell (2007), 'Is evil action qualitatively distinct from ordinary wrongdoing?', *Australasian Journal of Philosophy*, 85: 659–77.

Philosophers who have tied evil action to feelings of horror include:

Stephen de Wijze (2002), 'Defining evil: Insights from the problem of "dirty hands"', *The Monist*, 85.2: 210–38.

Marcus Singer (2004), 'The concept of evil', *Philosophy*, 79: 185–214.

Thinkers who explore the connection between evil and incomprehensibility include:

Simon Baron-Cohen (2011), *Zero Degrees of Empathy*, London: Penguin.
Adam Morton (2004), *On Evil*, New York: Routledge.
Luke Russell (2012), 'Evil and incomprehensibility', *Midwest Studies in Philosophy*, 36: 62–73.

Philosophers who claim that malice is a necessary condition for evil action include:

Laurence Thomas (1993), *Vessels of Evil: Slavery and the Holocaust*, Philadelphia: Temple University Press, see p. 76.
Manuel Vargas (2010), 'Are psychopathic serial killers evil? Are they blameworthy for what they do?', in S. Waller (ed.), *Serial Killers—Philosophy for Everyone: Being and Killing*, pp. 66–77, Oxford: Wiley-Blackwell, see p. 75.

Philosophers who claim that sadistic pleasure is a necessary condition for evil action include:

Roy Perrett (2002), 'Evil and human nature', *TheMonist*, 85.2: 304–19.
Hillel Steiner (2002), 'Calibrating evil', *The Monist*, 85: 183–93.

Philosophers who claim that defiance is a necessary condition for evil action include:

Roy Perrett (2002), 'Evil and human nature', *The Monist*, 85.2: 304–19.
Marcus Singer (2004), 'The concept of evil', *Philosophy*, 79: 185–214.

Garrard's silencing account of evil is found in:

Eve Garrard (1998), 'The nature of evil', *Philosophical Explorations*, 1: 43–60.

Morton's account of evil can be found in his book:

Adam Morton (2004), *On Evil*, New York: Routledge.

Arendt's analysis of Eichmann appears in her book:

Hannah Arendt (2006), *Eichmann in Jerusalem*, New York: Penguin.

Criticism of Arendt's claims about Eichmann can be found in:

David Cesarani (2004), *Becoming Eichmann: Rethinking the Life, Crimes, and Trial of a 'Desk Murderer'*, London: De Capo Press.

Bettina Stangneth (2014), *Eichmann before Jerusalem*, New York: Vintage.

Philosophers who have defended the view that evil actions can come from a very broad range of motives include:

Todd Calder (2002), 'Towards a theory of evil acts: A critique of Laurence Thomas's theory of evil acts', in Daniel Haybron (ed.), *Earth's Abominations: Philosophical Studies of Evil*, pp. 51–61, New York: Rodopi.

Claudia Card (2002), *The Atrocity Paradigm*, New York: Oxford University Press.

Paul Formosa (2008), 'A conception of evil', *The Journal of Value Inquiry*, 42: 217–39.

Susan Neiman (2003), *Evil in Modern Thought*, Melbourne: Scribe.

Luke Russell (2014), *Evil: A Philosophical Investigation*, Oxford: Oxford University Press.

Thinkers who are sceptical of the usefulness of the concept of evil include:

Simon Baron-Cohen (2011), *Zero Degrees of Empathy*, London: Penguin.

Inga Clendinnen (1998), *Reading the Holocaust*, Melbourne: Text Publishing.

Phillip Cole (2006), *The Myth of Evil*, Edinburgh: University of Edinburgh Press.

Lomax tells his story in the autobiographical book:

Eric Lomax (1995), *Railway Man*, New York: Vintage.

Aggregative and Dispositional models of evil personhood are explored in:

Luke Russell (2010), 'Dispositional accounts of evil personhood', *Philosophical Studies*, 149: 231–50.

The idea that the evil person is the mirror image of the virtuous person is defended in:

Peter Brian Barry (2011), 'In defense of the mirror thesis', *Philosophical Studies*, 155: 199–205.

Daniel Haybron (2002), 'Moral monsters and moral saints', *The Monist*, 85.2: 260–84.

Levi's account of his internment by the Nazis can be found in his book:

Primo Levi (1989), *The Drowned and the Saved*, trans. Raymond Rosenthal, New York: Vintage.

The fixed dispositional account of evil personhood is defended in more detail in:

Luke Russell (2014), *Evil: A Philosophical Investigation*, Oxford: Oxford University Press.

Milgram describes his experiments in:

Stanley Milgram (1974), *Obedience to Authority*, New York: Harper and Row.

The philosophical implications of these experiments are explored by Doris in his book:

John Doris (2002), *Lack of Character: Personality and Moral Behaviour*, Cambridge: Cambridge University Press.

Index

For the benefit of digital users, indexed terms that span two pages (e.g., 52–53) may, on occasion, appear on only one of those pages.

Evil

Evil